The
Women
of
Galway
Jail

The Women of Galway Jail

Female Criminality in Nineteenth-Century Ireland

Geraldine Curtin

Arlen House
2001

First published in June 2001 by

Arlen House
PO Box 222
Galway
Ireland

and

42 Grange Abbey Road
Baldoyle
Dublin 13
Ireland

www.arlenhouse.ie

ISBN   1–903631–12–2, hardback
        1–903631–11–4, paperback

Typesetting: Dunleavy Design, Galway
Cover Design: Dunleavy Design, Galway
Printed by: ColourBooks, Baldoyle, Dublin 13

Contents

List of Illustrations

Acknowledgements

The generous and gracious manner in which so many people have helped me in the preparation of this book has been a frequent source of surprise and delight to me. If the adage about the 'cheerful giver' is true, the following is a list of people who are truly blessed.

I am indebted to the staff of the National Archives and of the Galway County Library, especially Maureen Moran, for the help they have given me in my research. I am also grateful to my colleagues at the James Hardiman Library, NUI, Galway for their forbearance, help and encouragement.

For their generosity in allowing me to use photographic material, I thank Mrs. Grace Semple, Mrs. Maeve Frost and Tom Kenny. Thank you to Maureen Langan-Egan, Niamh Darcy, the *Connacht Tribune* and John Flatley for the use of research and archive material.

This book began its life as a dissertation for an M.A. in History and Local Studies at the University of Limerick. Dr. Bernadette Whelan was always a constructive and encouraging mentor.

Numerous friends have helped along the way, including Eileen, Ted, Diane, Mike and particularly Kieran who proof-read the manuscript. Valerie at Dunleavy Design was patient and professional above and beyond the call of duty.

Finally, thank you to Alan at Arlen House, without whom there would be no book.

Preface

Some years ago, a friend drew my attention to the census return for the Galway workhouse in 1901. Listed amongst the paupers who were resident there on the night of Sunday 31st. March were two women, 'M.W.' and 'M. O'N.' One was aged sixty, the other seventy. Under the heading 'Rank, Profession, or Occupation', both were listed as prostitutes. The census enumerator also recorded that both were in the workhouse because they were 'unable' to follow their usual occupations. Needless to say, my curiosity was aroused, and I wondered about the lives that these women had led in late nineteenth century Galway.

Two years ago, I began the research which has culminated in the publication of this book. I discovered that the registers for Galway's jails for every year, from 1st.January 1839 to 20th. April 1939, still exist. Amongst the thousands of women whose details were entered in these registers, I found many like 'M.W.' and 'M. O'N.' Theirs, I felt, was a story waiting to be told.

Notes: Many of the records used in the research for this book, such as the prison registers and the newspapers, gave the full names and addresses of prisoners, defendants and witnesses. However, only the first names and the initial of the surname (for example, 'Mary W.') have been used in this book.

'Gaol' is a variant spelling of 'jail'.

The
Women
of
Galway
Jail

INTRODUCTION

The majority of men and women imprisoned in Ireland in the nineteenth century served out their sentences in local prisons. In 1877 there were thirty-eight such prisons in this country, many of which were located in provincial towns such as Sligo, Castlebar, Roscommon, Ennis and Galway. The prisoners who were sent to these jails during this period were usually petty criminals found guilty of minor offences at the petty sessions courts by the local magistrates. More serious offenders were held in local jails while awaiting trial, and, once sentenced, were sent to convict prisons in Cork, Limerick or Dublin. Tens of thousands of men and women were sent to these local jails every year. Between April 1878 and March 1879, for example, over 45,000 people, one third of whom were women, served sentences in these thirty-eight prisons.[1] In the latter half of the nineteenth century, female criminals made up between one-fifth and a half of the overall prison population, both nationally and regionally.

In Galway, there were 3,577 admissions of women prisoners to its jail between 1878 and 1892. Some of these women were committed to the jail ten or more times a year. By 1892, however, admissions of females to the jail had halved, and female criminality in Galway, as elsewhere, was becoming less common. The aim of this book is to look at the women who were imprisoned in Galway in this period, at who they were, at the crimes they committed, and at how they were treated while in prison. A brief history of the prison as it pertained to women is also included, as is an overview of women in Galway during this period.

A key primary source used in this study is the prison register. These registers provide detailed descriptions of all prisoners who entered the jail, from the colour of their eyes to the crimes for which they had been committed. Official papers, such as the reports of the inspectors of prisons and judicial statistics, are a useful source of information for the administration of the prison and of the justice system. Contemporary local newspapers like the *Galway Express* and the *Galway Vindicator* gave accounts, often very detailed, of the petty and quarter sessions in much the same way that provincial newspapers report on court cases today. These accounts are usually the only opportunity we have to hear the voices of the potential prisoners. This is an unfortunate lacuna in the study of nineteenth century criminality. We rarely hear the voice of the real subject of the study – the woman who was arrested for prostitution, or drunkenness, or for abandoning her children. The tone of the newspaper accounts was often either satirical or unsympathetic. Court reports in the newspapers with titles like "How they live at the Small Crane", "Buttermilk Lane life" and "Cross Street again" were obviously intended for their entertainment value rather than as hard news. This gap in source material not only makes any meaningful study lacking in balance, but also makes an analysis of the causes of crime incomplete. We will probably never know, therefore, why women like "Bridget F.", part of whose story is told in this book, became prostitutes. However, the wealth of extant sources available has made it possible to look at Galway's women criminals in some detail.

"MARGARET N."

Age: 30
Crime: Murder

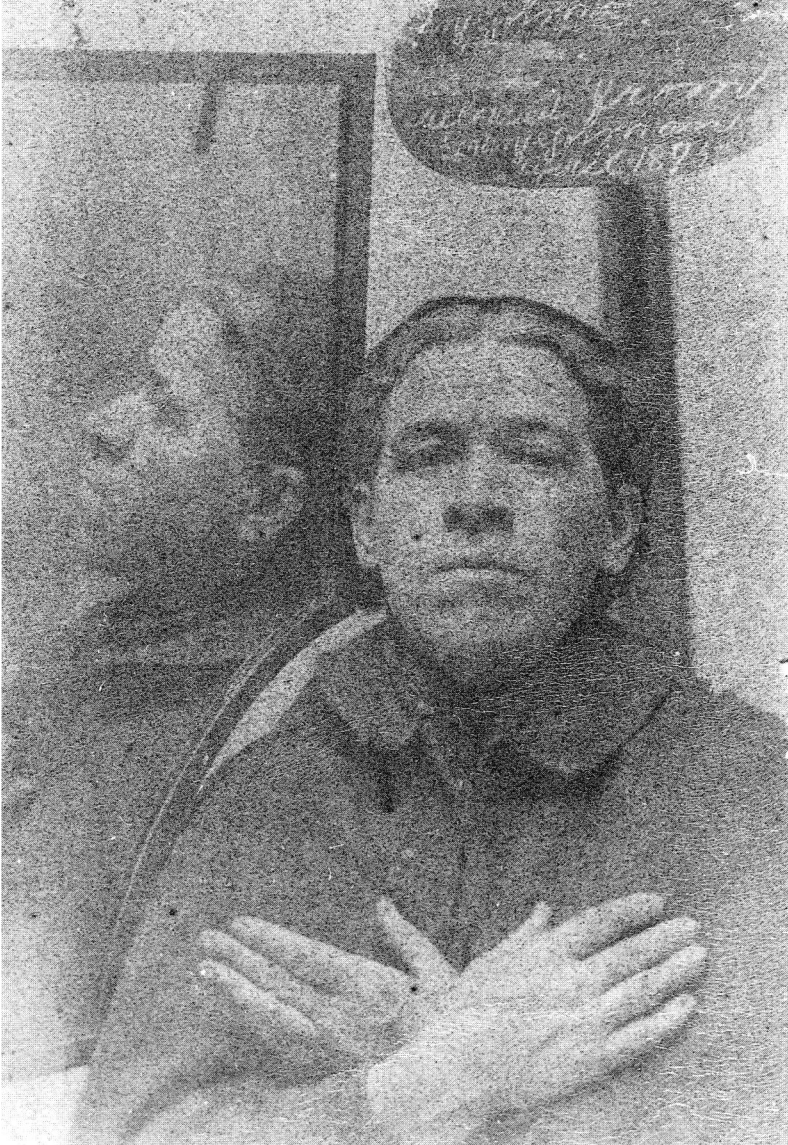

"Margaret N." was a single woman who was found guilty of murder in 1885. Described in the prison records as "stout and strong", she had been living in rural Galway with her brother, their nephew [newspaper accounts described him as their cousin] and his wife when the crime occurred. She was sentenced to fourteen years penal servitude and was transferred from Galway jail to Grangegorman convict prison in December 1885. Her brother, William, was convicted of the same crime, and was sent to Mountjoy, and later transferred to Cork jail. In a letter from the Governor of Galway jail to the Superintendent of Grangegorman, the circumstances of the crime were described as follows:

> The murdered man was an illegitimate and Nephew to the prisoners in whose house he and his wife resided, having obtained half the little farm.

Margaret appealed to the Lord Lieutenant and the Chairman of the General Prisons Board for early release, on the grounds of "strong provocation" when she committed the offence. She was initially refused, but was later recommended for early release by the Superintendent of Grangegorman, who said that "her conduct and industry remain very satisfactory", except for one occasion when she was involved in "wrangling with another convict in 1892".

Margaret was hopeful that she and her brother would emigrate to America on their release. She wrote to her sister in Essex County, Massachusetts in 1894, and received a cheque from her for four pounds. She wrote the following letter to her brother in jail in December 1894:

My dear Brother

I received your letter in due time. I was very sorry to hear that you were suffering from Rheumatism hoping you are better by this time, I am in good health thank God, I wrote to Ellen and explained every thing to her as you desired, I am very happy to know you heard from Mr. Walsh of late, and that he has your house and land waiting for you, did he make any mention of the expence [sic] in fencing in your half of the land since the first time, I remember one time you wrote to me saying that Mr. Walsh stated it would cost 20 pounds to make the fences and that you would give him the 20 pounds when you would get out or your land, it would not be an easy matter for us to make up 20 pounds after coming out of Prison and it would grieve me very much to see you hand your land over to any man on that condition, if you feel your health is strong enough would you not think it better for us both to go and earn a little capital before returning home you need make no arrangements as Mr. Walsh held it for the last 9 years he will hold it for one 12 months and that will give us a fair trial if the climate agrees with our health and if not we will be glad to have it, to return to it, as I expect to be discharged in April if you sent (an) [sic] a petition they might have mercy on you and have you discharged with me, it would be a very hard trial on me to go either home or abroad without you, may God direct to the best, let me know how your health is and also what you think is best for us to do, let me know in this next letter all particulars, as it would be too late again to make arrangements. I wish you a very happy Xmas

I remain your loving sister

"M."

Margaret was released on licence in April 1895, and subsequently emigrated. The records do not state whether her brother emigrated with her.

H. M. Prison
Grange Gorman
5th Decr 1893

Sir

I beg to request a report
from you, for the information
of the General Prisons Board
on the character and manner
of life of the undermentioned
convict prior to Conviction
she being committed to your
Prison, and tried at the
Connaught Winter assizes
Held at Sligo. in Decr 85

Name   Margaret ████████
Crime   Murder
Sentence 14 years P. S.
Date & Place. 21st Decr 1885
of Conviction   Connaught winter assizes
                Held at Sligo

        I am
        Sir
        Your obedient Servant
Governor   C. S. McCarthy
H.m Prison   Superintendent
Galway

8

H.M. Prison Galway
13 Dec. 1893.

Madam,

  I am informed by the constabulary of the district from which Margaret ▓▓▓▓ was committed that prior to her arrest for this crime she was of good character. She resided with her brother Wm. ▓▓▓▓ who was also convicted of the same offence, and assisted the latter in the management of a small farm.

  The murdered man was an illegitimate and Nephew to the prisoners in whose house he and his wife resided, having obtained half the little farm.

  It was a family dispute which led to the perpetration of this murder.

  I am,
  Madam,
Your obedient Servant.

Rob. Coutts.
Governor.

The Superintendent
H.M. Prison,
Grangegorman

9

Photograph, with statemen

(1̶

Photo on Reception

Relea
H. M.
Fran
on ac
on th
and
Emig

C.
Su

eference to final disposal.

Photo on Release on K.C.

7)

from
rson
gorman
e of 4 $\frac{244}{365}$ yrs
th aple 95.
ued to
te

Mc Carthy
tendent
9 : 4 : 95.

11

A GALWAY MURDER CASE

William N█ and Margaret N█ were then put upon their trial upon the charge of having murdered their cousin, Peter N█.

Mr Nolan, Q.C. and Mr Trench (instructed by Mr O'Farrell, Crown Solicitor, Galway,) prosecuted.

The prisoners were defended by Mr Tyler, B.L. and Mr Rynd, B.L (instructed by Mr Bowles.

Mr Nolan stated the case for the Crown. Informing the jury that the number of witnesses to be examined would be few. The prisoners and the deceased were cousins, and occupied a small house of three rooms—two bedrooms and a kitchen. One of the bedrooms was occupied by the deceased and the other by the prisoners. They appeared to occupy adjoining land, as to the possession of which there were some disputes. On the 7th of August the police were at the place about some dog license, and on that occasion the police heard the parties disputing, and they also heard the prisoner say he would fight for the possession of the land. The police sergeant advised them to settle their dispute. On the morning of the 8th a dreadful occurrence took place. The deceased, his wife, and mother-in-law, and sister-in-law were in the house. The deceased was standing outside watching a pig feeding, and suddenly his sister-in-law, Lizzie M█ heard a scream. She rushed out, and saw the male prisoner striking the unfortunate deceased with a stone. That was not the worst, but he was sorry to have to tell the jury that the female prisoner not alone stood by, but struck the deceased with a dreadful weapon, a soda water bottle enclosed in a stocking. The unfortunate deceased managed to crawl to his room, but the male prisoner followed him, and again beat him with a stone, and afterwards the matter was reported to a magistrate; but when the magistrate arrived at the house poor Peter N█ was lying dead in the room. The prisoners were charged with having murdered the man. Counsel called on the jury to give the case their serious attention. Of course if the evidence was not sufficient to prove the charge of murder, the jury could return a verdict of manslaughter. It was a case that required their most serious attention, as there was no doubt a life had been taken in a dreadful manner.

Several witnesses having been examined.

Counsel for the prisoners asked permission to hold a consultation with the prisoners.

His Lordship allowed it.

Mr Rynd and Mr Tyler Frere said that, acting on their advice, they did not resist the case further than to have the charge reduced to one of manslaughter.

Mr Nolan said the Crown would, under the circumstances, accept a verdict of manslaughter.

His Lordship said he had a duty to discharge irrespective of counsel for the prisoner or for the Crown. His lordship briefly charged the jury leaving it to them to decide the question.

The jury brought in a verdict of manslaughter.

Galway Vindicator & Connaught Advertiser, 23 December 1885.

chapter one

THE WOMEN

"Notorious bacchanalians" and nymphs of
"nocturnal propensities"

Introduction

In 1881, there were three hundred and fifteen admissions of women prisoners to Galway jail. In 1891, there were one hundred and sixty-nine. Almost all of these women were sent to prison for committing petty crimes such as minor assaults, petty theft, obscene behaviour, or for being drunk and disorderly. Some were frequent "guests" in the jail and their names appear in the registers on an almost monthly basis. Those awaiting trial, or on remand for more serious offences, spent short periods in the jail. Once sentenced, longer terms of penal servitude were served out in convict prisons such as Grangegorman or Limerick jail. This chapter will examine the social and economic conditions, age, literacy levels and occupations of the women who were in Galway jail in the late nineteenth century, with particular emphasis on two years, 1881 and 1891.

Women in late nineteenth century Galway

In 1851, there were 164,549 females living in County Galway. Women outnumbered men by 7,500. Over the next fifty years, however, more than 100,000 women and female children would emigrate from the county, so that by 1901, there were more men than women living in Galway. [2]

Population of County Galway, 1851–1901

Census Period	Persons	Males	Females
1851	321,684	157,135	164,549
1861	271,478	134,057	137,421
1871	248,458	122,496	125,962
1881	242,005	120,609	121,396
1891	214,712	108,283	106,429
1901	195,149	99,100	96,049

Late nineteenth century Galway was home to some of the poorest people in Ireland. In rural Galway, and in particular Connemara, a large proportion of the population lived on very small holdings. The poverty of west Galway was compounded by the occurrence of six famines between 1816 and 1882. The famine of 1879, caused by crop failure, was one of the worst and lasted for three years. Assisted emigration, whereby orphans and the destitute were given the means to emigrate, was seen by many as a solution to the problem. Assisted emigration was a contentious subject. Some saw it as an official attempt to purge Ireland of its poor, but there were those amongst the clergy, government officials and the poor who saw it as the best and only option for destitute people. J. H. Tuke visited Connemara in 1882 as a representative of a committee founded by the Duke of Bedford. The aim of this committee was to identify and put in place schemes to alleviate distress in the west of Ireland, including assisted emigration. He described scenes of abject poverty – families who could only afford a meal of stirabout every second day, and the case of a man who came to him for help and said that his wife and daughters were "naked in clothing and ashamed to come". Tuke stated that he received almost unanimous support for emigration schemes, and quoted a Connemara priest who said:

> I say with all the energy of my existence, Let the people leave in any and in every way that may take them out of the slough of poverty and misery in which they are at present sunk. [3]

While male emigrants outnumbered females almost consistently at national level up to 1891,[4] the figures for Galway show increasing numbers of women leaving as the century progressed.[5] From spring 1881, Allan Line steamers, bound for America, were leaving Galway every two weeks.

"ALLAN" LINE

ROYAL MAIL STEAMERS

SAIL REGULARLY FROM

GALWAY to BOSTON

AND FROM

GALWAY to PHILADELPHIA

carrying passengers at rates as low as those of any other first-class line. Passengers are booked through from

GALWAY TO NEW YORK

and to all the principal stations in the UNITED STATES and CANADA.

In these Steamers special attention is paid to

STEERAGE AND INTERMEDIATE

passengers. Stewardesses attend all female passengers, and an experienced surgeon is carried on each steamer.

The special attention of emigrants is drawn to these sailings, as from the position of Galway, these are undoubtedly the best routes from

IRELAND TO AMERICA.

Passengers also are carried weekly from Queenstown and Londonderry to Boston, Philadelphia, New York, Baltimore, Quebec, Montreal, Halifax, St. John's, &c.

For further particulars apply to

JAMES & ALEXANDER ALLAN,
70 Great Clyde Street, GLASGOW, and
11 Eyre Square, GALWAY;

or to their local agents.

Mrs. Fahy, 2, Bridge Street, Galway.
Mrs. Conroy, High Street, Galway.
P. L. Bodkin, Prospect Hill, Galway.
P. Mahon, Athenry.
John Roe, Oughterard.
Joseph Gorham, Clifden.

SAILINGS

GALWAY TO PHILADELPHIA

S.S. Prussian,	3,000 Tons	Thursday,	13th June

GALWAY TO BOSTON

S.S. Manitoban,	3,000 Tons	Sunday,	26th May.
S.S. Nestorian,	3,000	Thursday,	6th June.
S.S. Hibernian,	3,000	Saturday,	22nd June.
S.S. Manitoban,	3,000	Thursday,	4th July.

Of the women who remained in Galway, fewer were getting married. Census records give a statistical account of the "conjugal condition of females aged from 15 to 45 years". In 1881, 54.5 per cent of Galway women in this age group were unmarried.[6] By 1891, this had risen to 60.9%.[7] Widows and single females accounted for 73.63 percent of the total female population of the county by 1901.[8] A contributory factor to this change is the fact that prospective husbands sought larger dowries than their earlier counterparts, and many parents were reluctant, or unable, to pay. A further reason for the decline in marriage was the absence of marriageable men. The young and strong had emigrated, and many of those who were left lived on holdings so small that they could not have supported a family. Without the prospect of a husband to support her, a single woman's survival depended largely on her own initiative, experience and education.

Educational reform in late nineteenth century Ireland led to a dramatic increase in literacy levels throughout the country. Although Connacht continued to have by far the highest rates of illiteracy in Ireland throughout this period, the percentage of people in the province who could neither read nor write dropped from 72 percent in 1841 to 27 percent in 1891.[9] However, County Galway continued to have more people who were illiterate than any other county. In the census of 1881, for example, 25.2 percent of the population of Ireland could neither read nor write. The corresponding figure for Galway county and town was 45.87%.

Throughout Ireland, the educational gap between men and women narrowed, particularly after the Powis

Commission report of 1870. Implementation of the recommendations of this report meant that almost every Irish child born after 1870 could expect to have basic literacy and numeracy skills by the time they reached adulthood. However, children of the very poor and orphans were still likely to be disadvantaged. There were ten workhouse schools in Galway in 1879, with six hundred and ten pupils on their roll-books. Workhouse girls were taught skills which would enable them to gain employment in domestic service, and orphan girls from Galway workhouses were sent to St. Paul, Minnesota as part of assisted emigration schemes.

Opportunities in domestic service, traditionally one of the biggest employers of women in the nineteenth century, declined as the century drew to a close. In Galway in 1871, for example, there were 35,668 females engaged in this type of work.[10] By 1901, there were only 4,838 females in this class in the census.[11] While in other urban centres this gap was, to some degree, filled by the existence of manufacturing industry, very few such opportunities existed for the women of Galway. In 1881 *Thom's Directory*[12] referred to the manufacture of coarse linens and woollen stockings as being two of the principal occupations of the rural inhabitants of Galway, and noted the establishment of a linen-weaving factory at Oughterard. The principal manufactories of Galway town were:

> a brewery, distillery, paper-mill, foundry, tan-yard, several flour-mills, a clog-factory and a bag-factory.[13]

Many Galway women were street-traders, or "hucksters", "hawkers" or "dealers"". They sold a variety of goods, including eggs, milk, potatoes, fruit, tin-ware, periwinkles and woollen stockings. The women of the Claddagh sold the fish caught by their husbands, fathers and brothers in the fish market at the Spanish Parade. Others were publicans, running either licensed premises, or unlicensed, illegal shebeens. All of these women were somewhat unusual for the period, in that they were self-employed and, while not rich, were relatively financially independent.

SKETCHES FROM IRELAND: SPINNING NET THREAD IN THE CLADDAGH, GALWAY.

The number of female inmates in Irish workhouses outnumbered that of males in every census year from 1871 to 1901. On 24 February 1883, the ratio of male to female inmates in the Galway town workhouse was 189:283. In the county as a whole, it was 946:1169.[14] Amongst the 1169

Claddagh Turf Market, 1893

women in the Galway workhouses, there were 88 "Unmarried Women having, or known to have had" children. Thirty-seven of the 88 women in this category are listed as having more than one child.[15] For those women who did enter the workhouse with children, the possibility of losing them was very real. Eighty-six children under the age of twelve died in the workhouses of Connacht in 1881.[16] Many women who were destitute became criminals, and it is predominantly from the ranks of the very poor and the economically marginalised that Galway's female criminal population was drawn.

Committals to Galway jail 1878–92

Year	Males	Females
1878–79	803	336
1879–80	1055	351
1880–81	1114	437
1881–82	1152	370
1882–83	988	245
1883–84	699	268
1884–85	601	269
1885–86	652	215
1886–87	631	215
1887–88	777	206
1888–89	763	155
1889–90	656	177
1890–91	636	167
1891–92	556	166

Age

In June of 1891, a child of nine, "Mary F.", served a one-month prison sentence in Galway jail. Her crime was "larceny of money". While Mary was certainly one of the youngest female prisoners to serve a sentence in the jail in the late nineteenth century, she was not the youngest child to spend time in one of its cells. Sentenced along with Mary for the same crime was her mother, Margaret, who brought with her her female infant. This was not uncommon at the time, and many mothers entered the gates of the prison with their infant children in their arms, particularly when they were nursing them.

The very old, as well as the young, were not spared imprisonment. In December of the same year, a ninety-four year old woman named "Catherine H." was sentenced to three calendar months for "having illicit spirits". Her sentence was later commuted, no doubt due to her age.

In 1881, the average age of Galway's women prisoners was thirty-three. By 1891, this average had risen to thirty-seven and a half. Female criminality became less common as the century drew to a close, and younger women were less likely to be found in the jail. Many of the repeat offenders, or recidivists, were older women. By census night in April of 1901, only four of the twenty-three women in the jail were under the age of thirty. On the same night, there were four prostitutes in the Galway city workhouse, one of whom was seventy, and another sixty.

Literacy

Census statistics for Ireland show a dramatic increase in literacy in the latter half of the nineteenth century. In Connacht, the number of illiterate females over five years of age fell from 53.6 per cent in 1871 to 28.8 per cent in 1891. The prison registers recorded the education levels of all prisoners under three categories; "read and write", "read only" and "nil". While Galway's women prisoners showed a slight increase in literacy levels between 1881 and 1891, the standard of education attained by them is dramatically lower than that of the female population in general.

Literacy levels of women in Galway jail in 1881

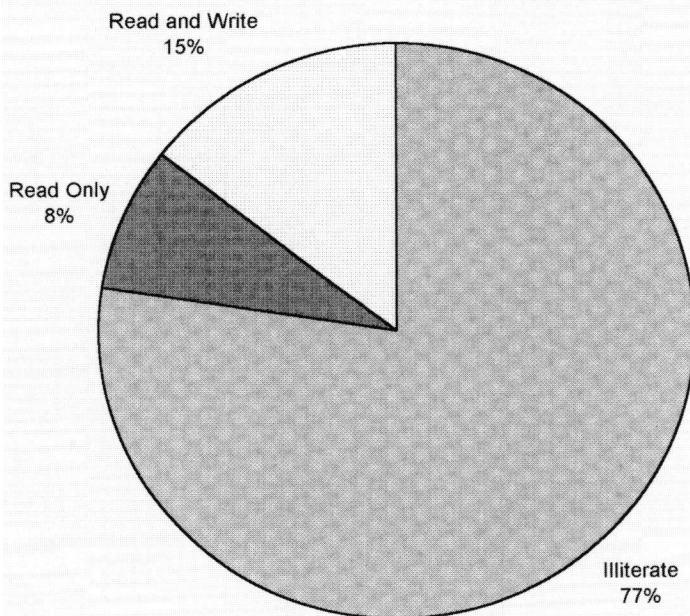

Read and Write
15%

Read Only
8%

Illiterate
77%

Seventy-seven percent of the women in the jail in 1881 could neither read nor write, and literacy among the female prison population had only improved by 7 percent ten years later.

The General Prisons Board had responsibility for the administration of Irish prisons from 1877. Their annual reports frequently cited "ignorance" and illiteracy as causes of crime and recidivism. They provided a framework for the education of prisoners, and schooling was part of every

Literacy levels of women in Galway jail in 1891

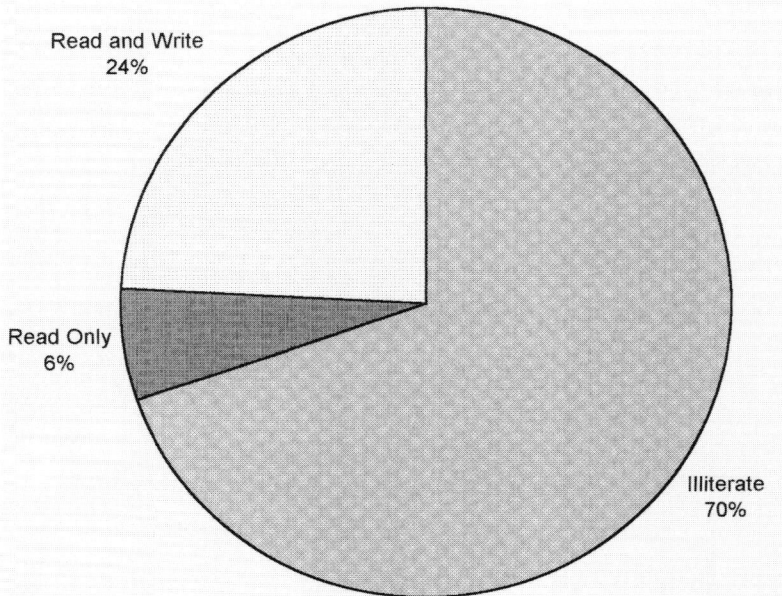

Read and Write
24%

Read Only
6%

Illiterate
70%

prison's daily schedule. Prison reformers such as the Quaker, Elizabeth Fry, recommended the separation and classification of prisoners and the introduction of structured sentencing whereby prisoners earned privileges like education and access to books as they progressed through their sentences. However, the reality of prison life did not always reflect official aspirations. The short sentences imposed on the majority of women in Galway (usually between twenty-four hours and one calendar month) made any meaningful attempts to educate them virtually impossible. Since so many of the women imprisoned in Galway during this period were found guilty of alcohol-related crimes, it is probable that for at least part of their time spent in prison they were "recovering". They may not, therefore, have been in the best or most receptive frame of mind for schooling. Others may not have had any desire to be taught. Various studies have shown that those women who had skills, education and ambition were leaving Ireland in the last two decades of the nineteenth century.[17] Without education, and with a prison record, employment prospects for women in Galway in this period would have been very poor.

Trades and Occupations

The trades and occupations of all prisoners were recorded in the prison registers on admission. The majority of the women in the Galway registers were unskilled workers engaged in poorly paid or precarious trades as servants, hucksters, charwomen, labourers or prostitutes. On rare occasions, a skilled worker such as an embroiderer or post-mistress entered the jail. Some were listed as having two trades, for example "charwoman and prostitute", or "lace-worker and cooper". Others were defined by their husband's occupation, such as "blacksmith's wife" or "tinker's wife".

Trades and occupations of women in Galway gaol in 1881 and 1891

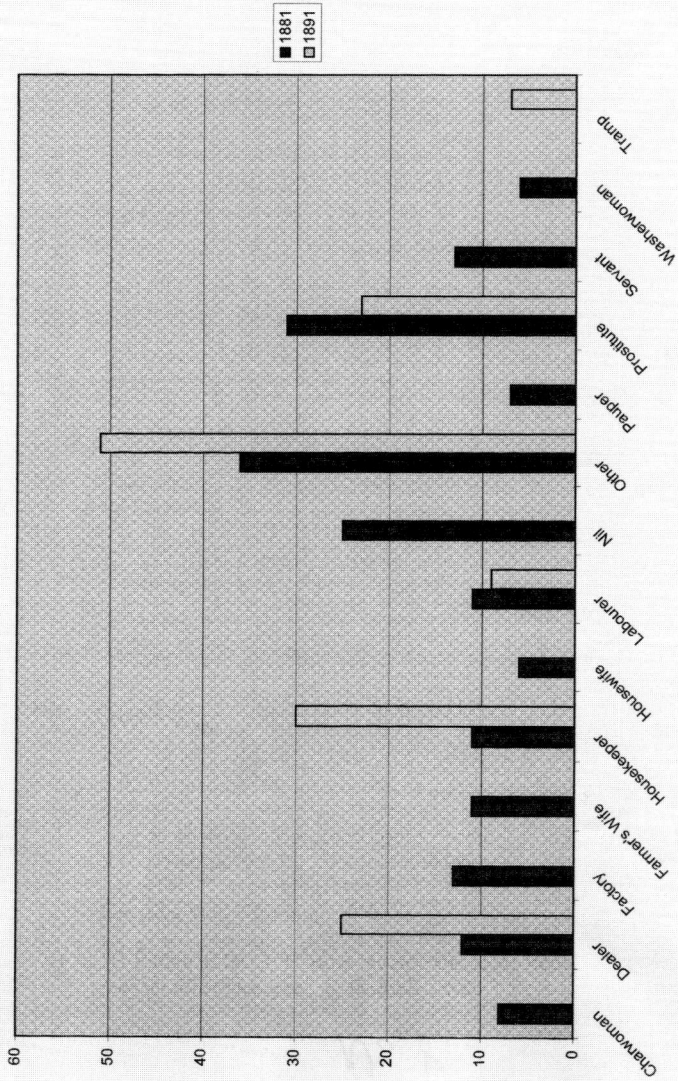

Legend: ■ 1881 □ 1891

Categories (left to right): Tramp, Washerwoman, Servant, Prostitute, Pauper, Other, Nil, Labourer, Housewife, Housekeeper, Farmer's Wife, Factory, Dealer, Charwoman

Y-axis: 0, 10, 20, 30, 40, 50, 60

Many of the women who were imprisoned and who made frequent appearances at the weekly petty sessions were "dealers". These women were street-traders and were also referred to as "hucksters" or "hawkers". In August 1881, a group of women appeared at the petty sessions on a charge of:

> obstructing the public thoroughfare by placing tables there for the sale of fruit, tin-ware &c.

The newspaper account of the trial described how:

> the tin-ware ladies, from the notorious Shell-lane and Boreenmeenough, let loose their tongues …

when the sentence of one shilling and costs was handed down. They were removed from court, but not before one of them:

> lifted her poor bare-footed *cosh* up to the magistrates and pointed out where a *boby* of a peeler, as she called him, kicked her.

She was found guilty of contempt of court, and was told by the magistrate that she:

> would not be allowed to turn the court into a beer-garden

and fined five shillings or a week in jail.[18]

Fowl market in Galway, 1893.

There were eleven housekeepers sent to the jail in 1881, and this number had risen to thirty by 1891. While the number of women engaged in domestic work declined considerably in this period, as did the number of women prisoners in general, it is interesting to note that the number of such women in jail tripled. The crimes for which they were sentenced in 1891 were predominantly drunkenness and assaults, which may reflect either the increased vigilance of the constabulary, or the frustration and despair of unskilled, poorly paid women with bleak employment prospects. A trade or occupation listed for the women in the prison register may refer to a post they had held in the past and does not necessarily mean that they were gainfully employed at the time of their arrest. In a curious case reported in *The Galway Express* in 1891, a young housekeeper was arrested for repeatedly throwing stones at the house of her former employer, who was a professor at Queen's College Galway. No explanation was offered for her behaviour, but she was described as "civil and obliging" and "perfectly honest and reliable". In the course of the trial, it transpired that she was in the employ of the magistrate trying the case, who defended his situation by stating that, had he not intervened, she would be "a jail-bird, whom no person would employ".[19]

Prostitutes, like drunkards, were frequently arrested for disorderly behaviour, drunkenness and for offences which came under the Vagrancy Acts. The Contagious Diseases Acts, whereby women believed to be prostitutes could be detained, inspected and treated for venereal diseases in a Lock hospital, were not enforced in Galway.

Some of these women had "prostitute" entered as their trade or occupation in the prison registers, but it is probable that there were others who were not listed as such. Judicial statistics include tables of "women of ascertained bad character", including prostitutes. According to the 1871 statistics, there were ten and a half thousand known prostitutes in Ireland, and sixty-five committals of such women to Galway county and town jails in that year. However, police and judicial statistics may not always represent an accurate picture of regional crime, particularly when it comes to prostitution. Part of the problem arises from the fact that these figures were compiled from data gathered by local police and were, therefore, dependant on the vigilance and accuracy of the local constabulary. For example, a newspaper account of a case of "shebeenism" from the Galway petty sessions in 1881 reported a constable describing the scene at a house in Middle Street. He entered the house and found "a marine and a female" sitting on a bed in a house which he described as a "training-house of ill-fame". On a subsequent visit, he found:

a soldier and a girl of ill-fame on the premises.[20]

In August of 1881, a police officer stationed in Galway, Constable Kehoe, described the Middle Street house as "the worst house in Ireland".[21] Yet in the categories of "Resorts of Thieves and Prostitutes" and "Other Houses of Known or Suspected Bad Character" in the judicial statistics for that year, Galway is reported as having no such premises.[22] In 1881 and 1891, approximately sixteen percent of the women who entered the jail were described as "prostitute" in the prison registers.

One small group of women who make frequent appearances in the jail registers are "beggars" or "tramps". The women who "took to the bag" in the nineteenth century were a common and accepted feature of everyday life. Somerville and Ross described the scene which awaited them as they left, or attempted to leave, a hotel in Eyre Square in 1890:

> On the pavement were clustered about us the beggarwomen of Galway – an awesome crew, from whose mouths proceeded an uninterrupted flow of blessings and cursings, the former levelled at us, the latter at each other and the children who hung about their skirts. We pushed our way through them, and getting up on the car announced that we were ready to start, but some delay in obtaining a piece of chord to tie up the breeching gave the beggars a precious opportunity. My second cousin was recognized, and greeted by name with every endearment.
>
> "Aha! Didn't I tell you 'twas her?"
> "Arrah, shut yer mouth, Nellie Morris. I knew the fine full eyes of her since she was a baby".
> "Don't mind them, darlin", said a deep voice on a level with the step of the car; "sure ye'll give to yer own little Judy from Menlo?"[23]

The women who begged did so for many reasons; their husbands may have deserted them or were migrant workers, their families may have been unable to look after them, or they may have been pregnant or with children and without the support of their families. Some, like the aforementioned Judy, were local, and others were migrant beggars and were referred to in the records as "tramps". The tramps were sometimes sent to jail in Galway for trying to gain admission to the workhouse out of their own Union area, but more often the crime of the beggars and tramps was that of "exposing their children" to suffering or danger. The passing of the Vagrancy Acts made begging or "wandering abroad without visible means of support" a criminal offence. Criminalization would eventually lead to its becoming less acceptable to the public and less "respectable" for those engaged in it. Those who begged or were vagrants risked a prison sentence.

The less common trades found listed in the prison registers include bag-maker, brush-maker, singer, milk-woman and rag-gatherer.

"Bridget F"

Age: 44
Crime: Robbery from the person

Bridget was a single woman who was described in the registers as a prostitute, and was originally from south county Galway. In 1885, she was sentenced to five years penal servitude in Grangegorman for robbery. By this time, she had had ninety-three previous convictions. Most were drunk and disorderly or obscenity charges, and she was a regular inmate of Galway jail in the 1880s. In 1880, she served one calendar month in Galway for "illegally using snares for taking hares and rabbits".

When sentenced in 1885, the official records state that Bridget had no residence, no next of kin, and, in a form sent from Galway jail in 1890, no "friends". In her two years in Grangegorman, Bridget sent one letter to a woman in Middle Street, but received none. She does not appear to have been troublesome, and was not punished for bad behaviour while in Grangegorman. As a result, she was transferred to Goldenbridge refuge, a "half-way house" for convict women in 1887. Bridget does not appear in the Galway prison registers by 1898–99. It is not known whether she had died, or moved, or was serving a sentence elsewhere.

Photograph, with statement in reference to final disposal.

Transferred to Golden Bridge Refm.

on 19th December 1887

E Nolte

Superintendent

29th Dec 87

chapter two

THE PRISON

"... such a terrible great height of a wall."[24]

The former town jail,
which became the female prison after 1884.

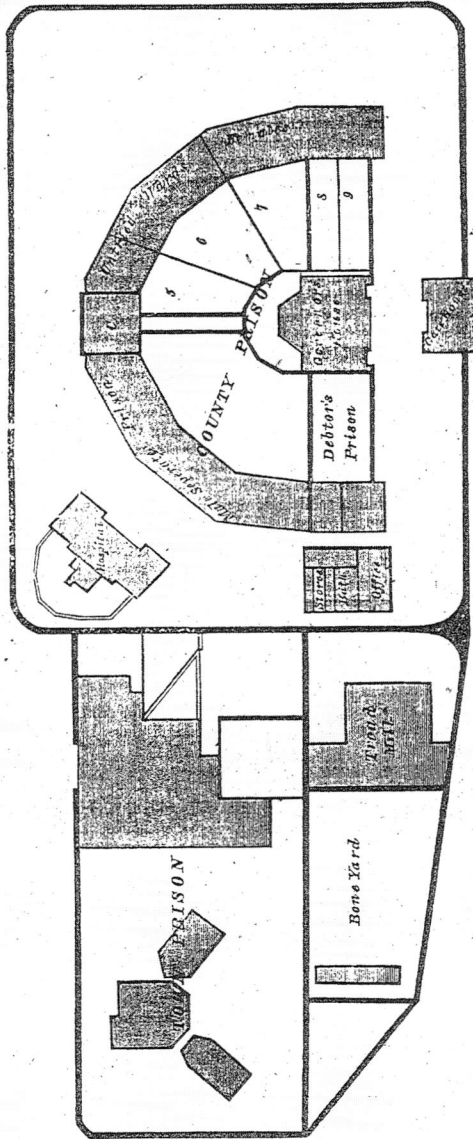

Plan of Galway jail,
from the Inspectors General Report of 1872.

Introduction

The late nineteenth century was a period of radical change in the prison system in both Britain and Ireland. The recommendations of philanthropic prison reformers such as Elizabeth Fry, John Howard and Mary Carpenter were influential in the early and mid-nineteenth century. In the last three decades of the century, however, it was largely scientific research and practical implications which influenced reform.

The General Prisons (Ireland) Act of 1877 established the General Prisons Board (GPB). The Act brought both local and convict prisons under direct government control, and sought to rationalize the prison system. Part of this rationalization included the introduction of comprehensive yearly inspections, a reduction in the number of prisons and bridewells, and a more uniform discipline structure. Some smaller prisons were closed down, and prisoners serving longer sentences were sent to convict prisons. This chapter will look at the history and administration of Galway jail and the conditions and day-to-day life of its women inmates between 1878 and 1900.

The main entrance to Galway jail.

History of the prison

Between 1804 and 1810 two jails were built on adjacent sites on Nuns' Island in Galway. One was the county jail and the other serviced the town. These prisons were administered by the Grand Jury and financed from the local cess, or tax. Prior to the building of the new prisons, criminals were incarcerated in the old town jail in Mainguard Street, the county jail in Blake's Castle and at various bridewells throughout the county. An inspector who visited Galway's jails in 1818 described the scene in a bridewell in the town:

> … the clanking of fetters, worn by ten wretched women, manifested its purpose; of these one had been confined twelve months, another eight, and the remainder several weeks.[25]

When the inspector asked the jailer to produce the committals for the women, he replied that they had been imprisoned on a verbal order of a local magistrate. The inspector ordered that the women be released and closed the bridewell.

Despite the building of the new prisons, subsequent inspectors' reports were often critical, particularly with regard to the town jail. The inspectors' report of 1831 referred to the "total neglect and melancholy state of the female prisoners" in the town jail, and recommended that the Grand Jury:

> remove this stain from the system of this town gaol, and … appoint a moral discreet matron who may be qualified not only to instruct the females in reading and work, but to watch over their moral conduct, and to introduce order and system in that class.[26]

In the county jail, they found prison discipline:

> to be in a most backward and almost wholly neglected state.

They finished their report on the county jail by expressing the hope that it would become:

> a scene of industry and general reformation to the well disposed, and of punishment to the idle and abandoned.[27]

Separation of prisoners was one of the changes which was recommended by some reformers, and the "separate system", whereby prisoners had no contact with each other at any time, had been established in many prisons. However, this could not be implemented in Galway as there were not enough cells. The report on the county jail in 1840 stated that there were only "… 98 cells in the whole prison for an average of 160 Prisoners", and went on to state that:

> The Females are only divided into two classes, and the accommodation for them by day and night is so confined, that no sound moral government can be carried on.

However, the inspectors did note that:

> the evil intercourse amongst Prisoners is considerably lessened by inspection during the day.

They also reported that there was a treadwheel for prisoners sentenced to hard labour, machinery for bone-breaking and that the prisoners were clothed in prison dress.[28]

Use of the treadwheel for prisoners was discontinued in most prisons by the 1870s, and, on the day of his visit, the inspector found the women in Galway engaged in carding, sewing, knitting and needle-work.[29]

Not surprisingly, conditions had deteriorated considerably by 1849. Prison diet, formerly stirabout, bread and milk, was reduced because "the superiority of the gaol dietary over that used in the workhouse" was inducing the poor to commit crimes in order that they would be sent to prison. In that year, the Inspector wrote:

> I shall not readily forget my first visit to the gaol of Galway. I cannot describe the wretched state in which I found its unfortunate inmates. Some of them half naked and without shoes, others clad in miserable and filthy rags and trembling with the cold.

The Governor, Mr. Ryan, and the local inspector, were both described by the Inspector General as humane, but powerless to ease the plight of the prisoners due to lack of finance. In 1848 and 1849, 11,697 prisoners had been admitted to the county and town jails.[30] In the same year the Inspector reported that a "paid schoolmaster" was employed by the prison, and that "those excellent and philanthropic ladies, the Sisters of Mercy" also gave "moral instruction" to the prisoners. The report for 1858 shows that there were 339 admissions of women to the town jail in the previous year, whereas the figure for men was only 255. Conditions for these women must have been very poor, as the Inspectors continued to be highly critical of the town jail. The women were divided into:

> three classes, mainly according to character, the prostitutes being kept apart from the others.[31]

However, meals were held communally, facilitating what the inspectors called "moral contamination". Work had finally begun on renovating part of the town jail to

TREAD-WHEEL AND OAKUM-SHED AT THE CITY PRISON, HOLLOWAY,

(WITH A DETACHMENT OF PRISONERS AT WORK ON THE WHEEL, AND THOSE WHO HAVE BEEN RELIEVED EMPLOYED PICKING OAKUM.)

accommodate the complete separation of women prisoners from the men. It was to be another twenty years, however, before this would be implemented. Between 1881 and 1884, the former town jail, which now had twenty-two cells, came to be used exclusively for women.

Staff

Despite the fluctuations in prisoner numbers, and the recommendations of prison reformers, there was very little change in staffing levels at Galway jail in the late nineteenth century, particularly with regard to female staff. There were between fifteen and twenty-four people employed in the prison between 1878 and 1892.[32] They included a Governor, a Chief Warder, two Chaplains, a "Surgeon/Apothecary", and a "Clerk/Schoolmaster/Schoolmistress". The warders were all male, and the only female staff members were either matrons, assistant matrons or servants. Although the campaigning of reformers such as Elizabeth Fry earlier in the century emphasised the need for female staff to attend to female prisoners, the ratio of women prisoners to staff remained largely unchanged in Galway. While there was provision for between two and four female employees working in the prison during this period (statistics for staff included vacancies), in some years there were only two members of staff who were women. They were usually a matron and an assistant matron. In some years there was a "female subordinate", and in two years, 1881 and 1892, there was no matron employed in the jail. It is to be assumed, therefore, that the male warders dealt with the women in matters of discipline, despite the fact that the 1859 Bill for consolidating and amending Laws relating to County Prisons in Ireland stipulated that "Female Prisoners shall in all cases be attended by Female Officers".[33]

Recruitment of suitable women into the prison service was a concern of the General Prisons Board, and in their fourteenth report in 1892 they stated that in Ireland:

> … the present staff of female officers is not at all what it should be.

It made its recommendations:

> … with a view to placing our officers more nearly on an equality with those in England, and so inducing young women of superior ability and position to enter our service.[34]

Wilfrid Scawen Blunt was a prisoner in Galway jail in 1888, and while his experience as a political prisoner was likely to have been very different from most ordinary criminals, he made some interesting comments about the prison warders. He noted that in the jail "… there had been a pleasant feeling" between the prisoners and warders, due to the fact that they:

> … were much of the same class, peasants born, with the same natural ideas, virtues, vices and weaknesses.

He described the effect of the visit of one of the afore-mentioned inspectors:

> The friendly warders were reprimanded and eventually dismissed … on charges of drunkenness (all prison warders in Ireland at that time were addicted to drink, and so easily dismissable).[35]

The impression given by Scawen Blunt is of a lax and far from harsh regime. Lucia Zedner, in her work on Victorian prisons in England, noted that:

> daily prison life was shaped largely by the inmates and warders who lived within its walls.[36]

This would certainly seem to have been the case in Galway. However, the General Prisons Board was keen to impose an orderly and disciplined structure on all aspects of prison life in the jails under its control.

Discipline

The winter time-table for prisoners began each day at 6.30 a.m. Peter Broderick, Secretary of the Athenry Land League, was held in Galway jail in 1881–82 as a political prisoner under the Better Protection of Persons and Property Act (PPP). He described the morning routine in a diary he kept while in prison. He was woken each morning by the bag-factory horn:

> … as the prison bells were ringing, it being almost dark. My cell door was opened. The gas put on. I dressed as best I could … about 20 minutes was allowed for this operation.[37]

The warders summoned the prisoners from their cells by calling "all out". A strict routine, in which exercise, eating, labour and schooling were scheduled, was set out by the General Prisons Board. While the general impression is one of order and discipline, the reality of prison life was probably not always so. In Galway, for example, there was no schooling of women prisoners between 1877 and 1888 despite the fact that school was scheduled into each weekday routine by the General Prisons Board.

Most prisoners who were able-bodied, both men and women, were sentenced to hard labour. The GPB sent every prison in its jurisdiction a "Classification and Labour Table". The classification system used by the General Prisons Board was very strongly influenced by the prison reformers of the early- and mid-nineteenth century. Prisoners were classified by their "moral character", the length of time they had spent in prison and by their behaviour. This system, the reformers believed, encouraged prisoners to work and had the added advantage of separating "incorrigible women" from those who might be reformed. As an inducement, prisoners were awarded "marks" which were accumulated in order to progress from one class to another and which could also be translated into money on a prisoner's release. This classification table divided prisoners into five groups, from probationers, through four grades to Class One. A probationary inmate in her first month of sentence could earn two marks a day by working at penal labour, for example oakum-picking, for ten hours. Her bed would have been a wooden plank, or plank-bed, and she would not have been entitled to gratuities, privileges (such as writing or receiving letters) or school. Once she had earned sixty marks, she could progress to Class Four. In Class Four, she would be required to work ten hours of "tasked" industrial labour, for which she would earn 4s. 2d. for every ten marks gained. She would be entitled to a slate, a secular book, school if

General Prisons Board, Ireland.

WINTER TIME TABLE,

To be enforced from 1st October in each year, to 31st March in the year following.

TIME TABLE of DAILY DUTIES in LOCAL PRISONS.

WEEK DAYS.		SUNDAYS.	
A.M.		A.M.	
6.30	Bell rings and prisoners rise, wash and clean cells, &c.	7.15	Bell rings; prisoners rise, wash, and clean cells.
6.45	Officers muster, and commence to Unlock.	7.30	Officers muster.
		7.45	Exercise or chapel.
7.0	Exercise.	9.0	Prisoners breakfast.
8.0	Labour commences.	9.10	Officers (except patrols) breakfast.
8.30	Prisoners breakfast.		
8.45	Officers (except patrols) go to breakfast.	10.15	Officers return; patrols go to breakfast.
9.30	Labour in cells recommences; patrols go to breakfast and officers return.	P.M.	
		1.0	Dinner.
P.M.		1.10	Officers (except patrols) go to dinner.
1.0	Dinners (prisoners'), school, and religious instruction.	2.15	Patrols relieved.
		2.20	Exercise.
1.10	Officers (except patrols) go to dinner.	3.0	In cells; officers (except patrols) go off duty.
2.0	Labour recommences, and patrols go to dinner.	4.45	Supper.
		6.45	Bed.
3.30	Exercise for such prisoners as the Governor may order.	7.0	Lights out.
4.30	Labour in cells.	10.0	Patrols relieved by night watch.
5.45	Supper, school, or religious instruction.		
6.30	Evening guard come on duty; labour recommences in cells.		
8.0	Bed.		
8.30	Lights out.		
10.0	Night watch come on duty.		

necessary and one visit. Privileges, such as the writing of letters, increased, and hours worked daily were reduced by one hour as the sentence progressed. Idleness and misconduct led to loss of marks and possible regression to a lower class, and to other forms of punishment. This classification system was, however, difficult to enforce in smaller local prisons, due primarily to the short sentences served by the majority of prisoners.

The Governor of each jail was obliged to submit a yearly return detailing work engaged in by prisoners. Much of the work done by the prisoners was related to the upkeep of the prison. Prison authorities at the time were sensitive to the hostility that could have been created by establishing moneymaking ventures which would have been seen as unfair competition by those outside the prison, particularly in an area of high unemployment like Galway. Prisoners were engaged in tailoring, tin-smithing, whitewashing, sewing and washing clothes and bedding, cooking, knitting and in nursing sick prisoners. The more traditional types of prison labour such as mat-making and the picking of coir and oakum also occupied prisoners of both sexes.[38] Prisoners were paid for these labours and could claim the money they earned on their release.

There were four categories of punishment permitted by the prison authorities for local prisons – irons or hand-cuffs, corporal punishment, punishment cells and dietary punishment. The offences which led to such punishment were also in four groups – violence, escapes and attempts to escape, idleness and "other breaches of regulations".

No. 2.—HARD LABOUR, FEMALES, UNDER RULES 24, 38, 39.

CLASSIFICATION AND LABOUR TABLE.

Class.	Penal Labour.	Industrial Labour.	Marks.	Relaxations.	Restrictions.
Probation,	10 Hours,	—	Can earn 2 Marks daily.	Nil.	Plank Bed without Mattress; no School; no Gratuity or other privileges.
Class 4,		10 Hours (tasked),	Ditto.	Slate; Secular Book; School (if necessary); Gratuity.	
Class 3,		10 Hours (tasked),	Ditto.	Slate; receive and write a Letter; two Books (Secular); School, if necessary; one Visit; increased Gratuity.	
Class 2,		9 Hours (tasked),	Ditto.	Slate; new Book every Month; two Visits; receive and write two Letters; increased Gratuity; Fatigues, if not sufficient in Class 1; School, if necessary.	
Class 1,		9 Hours,	Ditto.	Fatigues of the Prison; Letter written and received once in two Months; Visits once in three Months; new Books when required; Slate; School, if necessary.	

1st Month, 60 Marks to be gained before promotion to Class 4.

2nd and 3rd Month, in which 120 Marks to be gained before promotion to Class 3.

4th, 5th, and 6th Month, in which 180 Marks to be gained before promotion to Class 2.

7th to 12th Month, in which 300 Marks to be gained before promotion to Class 1.

Above 12 Months.

Misconduct and Idleness will entail loss of Marks and reduction in Class and Diet; and, if persevered in, the Prisoner will be returned to the Probation Class.

The Money value of Marks is as follows:—
For every 10 Marks gained in Class 4, 2d.   For every 10 Marks gained in Class 2, 3½d.   Until the expiration of two years, after which period each case will be considered.
Do.,   Class 3, 3d.   Class 1, 3½d.

PENAL LABOUR will consist of Oakum-picking (tasked), Hair or Wool-picking, with such other definitions as may from time to time be added by the Prisons Board.
The Conduct of Prisoners must be good in order to entitle them to receive Marks.
In Gaols which have not Prisoners in Classes 1 and 2, the selection for Fatigues will be made from those longest in the Prison, provided their conduct has been satisfactory.

51

Whipping and leg-irons had been abolished in the 1860s, and corporal punishment appears to have been in place for men only. From 1884, irons and cuffs were no longer used as a form of punishment.

According to the annual reports of the General Prisons Board, there were over ten times as many men as women found guilty of prison offences in Galway jail between 1878 and 1891 – 2,802 men and 241 women. However, the number of women punished for violent behaviour is proportionately much higher than the corresponding number for men. Twenty-eight men and twenty-five women were punished for violent behaviour in this period. In one year, there were eleven occasions on which women were punished for violence, and only two amongst the men.

From 1884, the General Prisons Board reports contained tables illustrating "Cases in which Mechanical Restraints have been used on prisoners in Local Prisons".

TABLE XIII.—RETURN showing Cases in which MECHANICAL RESTRAINTS have been used on PRISONERS in LOCAL PRISONS, IRELAND, during the year ended 31st March, 1886—*continued.*

NAME OF PRISON.	Sex.	Initials of Prisoner placed under Restraint.	Authorized mode of Restraint.	Reason for placing Prisoner under Restraint, specifying whether in Hospital or otherwise.	Period during which Prisoner was under Restraint.	Remarks.
Larger Prisons—con.						
Dundalk—con.				Not in hospital—		
	M.	J. McC.	Muffs.	Destroying prison property.	6 hours.	
	M.	J. B.	Handcuffs,	do.	2 hours.	
	M.	J. C.	Muffs,	To prevent him injuring himself.	5 hours.	
Galway,	M.	J. B.	Handcuffs,	Threatened suicide.	5 days and 7 nights.	
	M.	J. F.	do.	Violence, and assaulting warder.	½ an hour,	Sent to Lunatic Asylum.
	M	S. B.	do.	Smashed cell window and threatened suicide.	24 hours,	do.
	F.	B. B.	Muffs.	Violent,	4 hours,	Had been in Lunatic Asylum. Sent again to Lunatic Asylum.
				In hospital—		
	F.	B. F.	do.	Suspected intention of suicide.	24 hours.	
				Not in hospital—		
	F.	B. B.	do.	Violent,	17 hours,	Had been in Lunatic Asylum.
	F.	K. D.	do.	do.	18 hours,	Sent to Lunatic Asylum.
				In hospital—		
	M.	G. K.	do.	Violent, assaulting prisoners in charge of him.	17 hours and 5 nights.	Mental condition doubtful.
				Not in hospital—		
	F.	K. R.	do.	Violent, smashed cell window.	3½ hours.	
Grangegorman,	F.	M. M.	Leather muffs	To prevent violence,	24¼ hours.	
	F.	E. B.	do.	do.	¾ hours.	
	F.	E. B.	do.	do.	19 hours.	
	F.	M. R.	do.	do.	20 hours.	
	F.	M. M.	do.	do.	4 hours.	
	F.	L. M.	do.	do.	18 hours.	
	F.	L. M.	do.	do.	9 hours.	
	F.	L. M.	do.	do.	14 hours.	
	F.	B. C.	do.	do.	7½ hours.	
	F.	F. S.	do.	do.	20½ hours.	
	F.	C. S.	do.	do.	6½ hours.	

Female convict with restraints

Restraints, such as hand-cuffs, muffs, straps, belts and strait-jackets were used to prevent prisoners from committing acts of violence on themselves, others or prison property. Only muff restraints were used on women in Galway in the 1878– 1891 period, for between three hours and three days at a time. The reasons why they were so treated were usually because of violent behaviour, or attempted suicide. Two women prisoners attempted to assault an officer in 1889–90, and in 1887–88, prisoner "A.O." was restrained for a total of eleven days for violent behaviour, improper conduct in chapel, threatening suicide, breaking a cell window and tearing her clothes.[39] This was the same year in which the aforementioned eleven violent incidents took place, and it is possible to establish from the tables that five other women were restrained for violent behaviour in the same year, but not, however, whether these were for isolated incidents or a group effort.

Many of the women who were restrained would appear to have suffered from emotional or psychological disorders. Some were subsequently sent to Ballinasloe asylum from the jail, but their names frequently re-appear in the jail registers. While it may appear that these emotionally vulnerable women were treated harshly, the restraints used may have been the only means available to the prison staff of preventing a disturbed woman from harming herself.

The following Articles may be ordered as **Extras or Substitutes** in the quantities deemed necessary by the Medical Officer.

Ale.	Corn Flour.	Jelly.	Sago.
Bacon.	Eggs.	Lemonade.	Spirits.
Beef Tea.	Fruit.	Milk.	Stout.
Biscuits.	Greens (or other	Porter.	Sugar.
Butter.	Vegetables).	Potatoes.	Tea.
Cake.	Ice.	Poultry.	Waters (Mineral).
Cocoa.	Jam.	Rice (ground).	Wine.
Coffee.			

INSTRUCTIONS.

Rice Pudding,	2 ounces rice ; 1 pint milk ; 1 ounce sugar ; 1 egg and nutmeg, to produce 20 ounces.
Arrowroot,	1 ounce arrowroot; 1 pint milk ; 1 ounce sugar, to produce 1 pint.
Beef Tea,	16 ounces of the lean parts of the neck of the ox to 1 pint water.
Tea,	⅓ ounce tea ; ¾ ounce sugar ; 2 ounces milk, and water to make up ¾ pint.
Cocoa,	¾ ounce flaked or Admiralty cocoa to 1 pint water, sweetened with ¾ ounce molasses or sugar for flaked cocoa, and ½ ounce molasses or sugar for Admiralty cocoa.
Lemonade,	¼ ounce cream of tartar ; ½ lemon (sliced) ; 2 ounces loaf sugar ; water 1½ pint. The water to be added hot to the other ingredients, and the whole to be allowed to stand till cold ; then strain.
Mutton,	To be roast or baked on four days in the week, and boiled on three days. On the days on which the mutton is boiled the meat liquor to be thickened with ¼ ounce flour, and flavoured with ¼ ounce onions per diet

---

DIETS FOR ILL-CONDUCTED OR IDLE PRISONERS.

No. 1.—BREAD AND WATER DIET.

MEN AND WOMEN.

1 lb. Bread per diem, with Water.

This diet to be limited, in the first place, to 3 days ; after that, one of the undermentioned diets, according to labour performed, for 3 days before its repetition, when it is again to be limited to 3 days, and a second interval on one of the undermentioned diets is to elapse before it is again repeated. The entire period, including intervals, for which any single term of this diet may be ordered, is not to exceed 15 days. No task of labour is to be enforced on any one of the 9 days on which the bread and water constitute the sole food supplied to the prisoner.

No. 2.—STIRABOUT DIET.

For Men and Women performing a daily task of any labour not expressly defined as Hard Labour.

Breakfast,	. .	Bread, 8 ounces.
Dinner,	. . .	1 pint stirabout, containing 2 ounces oatmeal, and 2 ounces Indian meal, with salt. Potatoes, 8 ounces.
Supper,	. . .	Bread, 8 ounces.

This diet to be limited, in the first place, to 21 days; after that, the diet of the class to which the prisoner belongs, for 1 week before its repetition, when it is to be limited to 14 days. The entire period, including the interval, for which any single term of this diet may be ordered, is not to exceed 42 days.

No. 3.—FOR MEN PERFORMING A DAILY TASK OF HARD LABOUR.

Breakfast,	Daily,	1½ pint stirabout, containing 3½ oz. oatmeal, and 3½ oz. Indian meal.
Dinner,	Sunday,	1 pint meat soup, with 4 oz. beef without bone. Potatoes, 16 oz.
	Monday, Tuesday, Thursday, Saturday,	} Bread, 16 oz. Vegetable soup, 1 pint.
	Wednesday, Friday,	} Bread, 8 oz. Potatoes, 16 oz.
Supper,	Daily,	Bread, 10 oz. Cocoa, 1 pint.

This diet to be limited to 28 days; after that the diet Class 3 shall be resumed for 14 days, before its repetition. The Governor shall have authority to direct this dietary for any period not exceeding 28 days.

The foregoing rules shall apply to the prisoners confined in every ordinary prison, and shall come into operation upon the expiration of forty days after the same having been settled and approved by the Lord Lieutenant or Lords Justices and Privy Council, shall have been laid before Parliament.

Made and executed this 10th day of August, 1881, by "The General Prisons Board for Ireland."

CHARLES F. BOURKE, Chairman.

[Seal.]

By the LORD LIEUTENANT and PRIVY COUNCIL of IRELAND.

COWPER.

In pursuance of the General Prisons (Ireland) Act, 1877, We, the Lord Lieutenant-General and General Governor of Ireland, with the approval, advice, and consent of the Privy Council of Ireland, have settled and hereby approve of the foregoing rules made by the General Prisons Board for Ireland, with respect to the diets of the prisoners confined in ordinary prisons in Ireland.

Given at the Council Chamber, Dublin Castle, the 20th day of August, 1881.

O'HAGAN, C.   HENRY ORMSBY.

C

Health and Diet

Eleven prisoners died while serving sentences in Galway jail between 1878 and 1892. All of them were male, and nine of the eleven were executed. According to official figures, therefore, only two prisoners became fatally ill while serving sentences in the jail in a fifteen-year period, even though there had been an outbreak of typhoid fever in the town in 1891.[40] The General Prisons Board Inspectors reported annually on "Cases of Sickness and Lunacy" in each of the local prisons and noted "Particulars of each case of Insanity" amongst the prisoners. The latter reflected the concern of the inspectors that such prisoners should be sent to local asylums instead of prison. From 1885, the reports of the Inspectors gave details of prisoners released on medical grounds. From 1890 onwards a very detailed table of "Diseases for which Prisoners on Sick Registers have been treated" was included. This table contained a list of one-hundred and thirty-five diseases and the number of prisoners treated in each of the prisons for these conditions. Unfortunately, it did not specify whether the prisoners were male or female, but it does serve as a useful indicator of the general health of prisoners, and of the level of care afforded them.

Of the twenty-three prisoners released on medical grounds between 1885 and 1892, ten were women. Five of the ten were released due to pregnancy, either because they were near their confinement, or because they were in poor health. Prisoner "M.C." was released in July 1891 due to her "advanced pregnancy". Her crime was "exposing her children to unnecessary suffering". It would appear from the General Prisons Board reports that the prison authorities in Galway took a sympathetic view of sick prisoners. A male prisoner was released in April 1887 because he was "fretting and not eating food", even though he had only served two months of a six-month sentence for assault occasioning actual bodily harm. In 1891, a ninety-four year old prisoner, "C.H.", had her sentence commuted. She had been sentenced to three calendar months for having illicit spirits. After nine days in jail, she was released. The prison authorities described the circumstances of her release:

> This woman was discharged in consequence of commutation of her sentence after nine days' imprisonment during which she had to be fed on invalid diet, and was also ordered stimulants by the medical officer. On discharge she had to be accompanied home by a prison officer in a special covered conveyance.[41]

Despite the concerns of the General Prisons Board, the overall number of "lunatic" prisoners incarcerated in Galway increased rather than decreased between 1878 and 1892. However, this increase may reflect heightened awareness by prison authorities of mental illness amongst its inmates, since statistics had to be presented from 1884 showing the mental state of "insane" prisoners on reception, the type of insanity in each case and how the case was dealt with. The initials, age, crime, education levels and sentence of these prisoners are recorded, so that it is possible to make a reasonably positive identification of individuals. For example, "B.B.", a nineteen-year old prostitute suffering from "mania" and imprisoned for attempting suicide, was sent to Ballinasloe asylum in 1884.[42] The following year, "B. B.", a prostitute with "mania", aged twenty, imprisoned for assault and obscene language, was again sent to Balinasloe.[43] There can be little doubt that this was the same woman. In the same year, "K.D.", aged twenty-two, a prostitute suffering from mania, was sent to jail for obscene language and drunkenness.[44] Six years later, a prostitute named "K. D.", aged twenty-seven, was sent from Galway jail to Ballinasloe suffering from "dementia" with acute attacks of "mania".[45] Her crime was a suicide attempt.

Of the twelve cases of women who were removed from the prison and sent to Ballinasloe between 1878 and 1892, seven were listed as suffering from "dementia", three from "mania" and one from "amentia". It is most likely that the diagnosis of mental illness amongst prisoners was made by the prison surgeon/apothecary. How these prisoners were diagnosed and treated is not clear from existing records. Criminal psychology was the subject of vigorous research in the late nineteenth century, and a number of studies were conducted on criminal women. One of the best-known contemporary criminal psychologists was Caesar Lombroso. He wrote one of the first detailed studies of female criminal behaviour. He asserted that:

> Sensuality has multiple and imperious needs which absorb the mental activity of a woman …

More tellingly, perhaps, he stated that a:

> … characteristic of the female lunatic, and consequently of the criminal lunatic, is an exaggeration of the sexual instincts.[46]

That which was considered abnormal behaviour amongst women was frequently associated with expressions of sexuality.

The general health of the prisoners was, naturally, affected by their diet. For some, the prison diet was superior to their "normal" diet while at liberty. Prisoners were weighed on admission and release, and it is not unusual to find prisoners who had gained weight while serving their sentences. In 1867, a Committee was established to "… enquire into the Dietaries of County and Borough gaols in Ireland". They recommended a dietary of 7oz. of meal and half a pint of new milk for breakfast, and a dinner consisting of 12oz. of bread and fl of a pint of new milk for a female prisoner serving a hard labour sentence of a week or less. Longer sentences merited a better diet, which included vegetable soup and tea and bread for supper. Those serving sentences of a month or more would be entitled to meat soup on Sundays and Thursdays, and juveniles of both sexes were given extra rations. The surgeon of the Galway jails made a report to the Committee, stating that the dietaries in both jails were insufficient, and that prisoners in the county jail had to fast for eighteen hours, from 3 p.m. to 9 a.m. the following morning. Presumably, this referred to prisoners on short sentences. Their diet was very meagre, and was probably intended to be inferior to the workhouse diet in order to discourage people from committing petty crimes to gain access to jail. The recommended dietary set out by the Committee in 1867 appears to have formed the basis for prison diet in Ireland in the late nineteenth century, with a number of changes being added, such as the addition of extra rations for nursing mothers. In February, an advertisement was placed in *The Galway Vindicator* stating that:

> The G.P.B. will receive sealed tenders for supplying: Bread, white and brown; flour, best seconds; wheatmeal, oatmeal, Indian meal, potatoes, beef and mutton, vegetables, rice, tea, coffee, pepper, sugar, molasses, new milk, buttermilk, salt, etc. [47]

These provisions, while appearing to be quite substantial and varied, were probably intended for both staff and inmates. Had a cold and hungry woman living on the streets of Galway seen this advertisement and been able to read it, it might certainly have induced her to commit a crime such as the breaking of a window so that she might dine on beef and bread and buttermilk.

"Mary W."

Age: 20
Crime: Stealing a purse containing a certain sum of money and some pawn tickets.

Mary was from Galway city and was married with no children. The sight of her left eye was defective. Her "character before conviction" was "not good". She had been convicted at Galway assizes in 1876 on a charge of false pretences, for which she was sentenced to two months imprisonment. In 1881, she was found guilty of larceny, for which she served six months, and she had also served time for "picking pockets at Castlebar". In 1882, she was sentenced to seven years penal servitude in Grangegorman Women's Prison for stealing a purse.

While there, she "feigned insanity". The medical officer found her to be sane, but "flighty and excitable if annoyed". She was moved to Goldenbridge refuge. Once there, she threatened to commit some "great crime" and "kept everybody up" and attacked and "threatened to take the life of all the other women" if not sent back to Grangegorman. Her licencè was revoked in May 1887 and she was sent back.

Mary could not be taught to read and write while in prison due to her bad sight, although she sent letters to her husband and father. (A prison officer usually acted as scribe). When back in prison, she assaulted officers and other women, and used "filthy and abusive and threatening language". She was also punished for knocking on her cell door at night with a brush "demanding to be brought to a punishment cell". The medical officer, whose duties included ensuring that prisoners were fit for punishment, stated that muff restraints could not be used on Mary as her fingers had been bitten.

Photograph, with statement in reference to final disposal.

Transferred to
Golden Bridge Refuge
October 1st. 1886

To Miss ———
Superintendent
Grangegorman Prison
Discharged on Licence 24th Augt 1887
and sent to Galway.

W Armstrong
Deputy Gov?
August 23rd 1887

In July 1898, Mary appears in the Galway prison register serving a sentence for three charges of drunkenness and one of indecent behaviour. Her age, according to the register, is thirty-nine and a half, and she is "nearly blind".

chapter three

THE CRIMES

"... sacrificing at the shrine of the rosy god"

Introduction

The types of crime committed by women in late nineteenth century Galway usually came under the heading of "crimes against morals", as set out in the judicial statistics of 1871. Although this category is not clearly defined, drunkenness, obscenity, disorderly behaviour, and crimes that involved prostitution or alcohol usually fell under this heading in subsequent parliamentary reports. Many of the crimes committed by Galway women were alcohol-related. Drunkenness and crimes associated with alcohol were topics which were the subject of frequent debates by government officials, criminologists and psychologists in this period. Seventeen Bills and Amendments pertaining to "habitual drunkards" (that is, persons who were arrested for being drunk three times or more in one year) passed through the House of Commons between 1870 and 1900.

Many of the women who were incarcerated in Galway jail towards the end of the nineteenth century were recidivists, or repeat offenders.[48] An inspector who visited the jail in 1875 found that:

> one female was committed ten times, and nine others nine times during the year. One has been upwards of 120 times an inmate of this prison since her first committal.[49]

IRISH SKETCHES : MARKET WOMEN OF THE OLD BOOTHS, GALWAY.

"Kate C.", a vegetable dealer, was imprisoned in September 1881 for obstructing the public thoroughfare. In an examination of her records in court, the magistrate found that she:

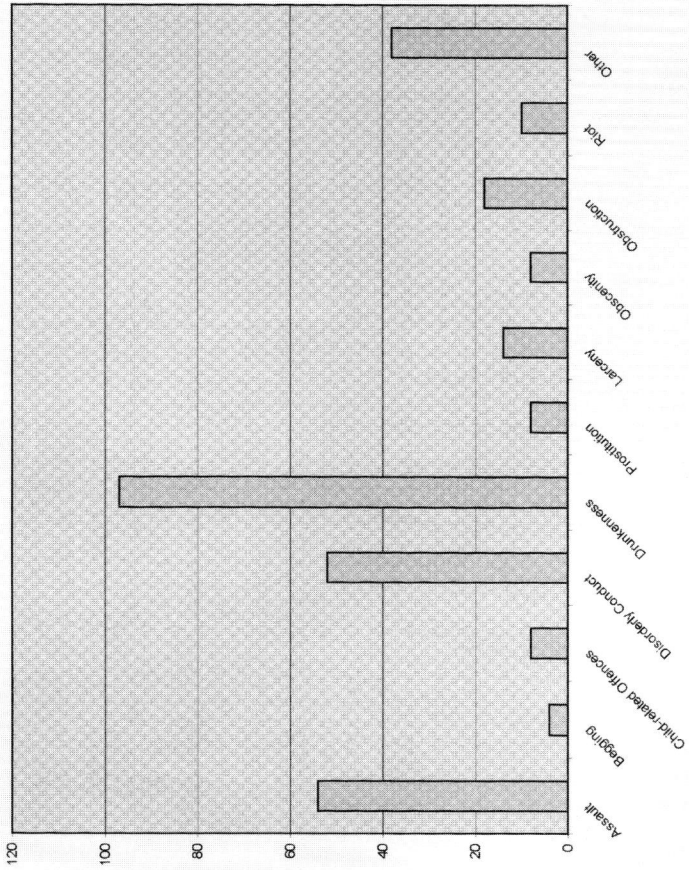

Crimes of women in Galway gaol in 1881

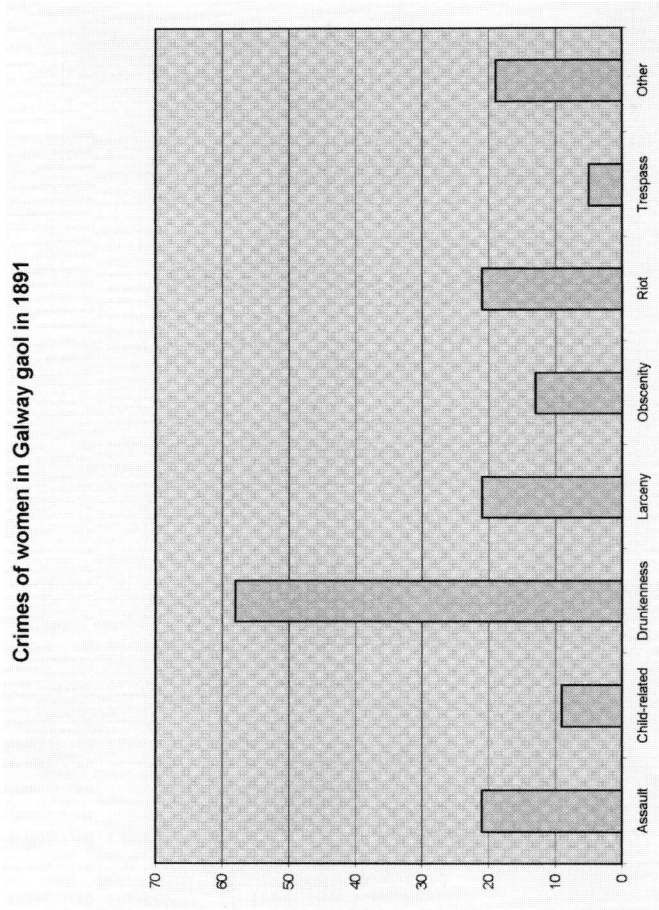

Crimes of women in Galway gaol in 1891

was shown to have been no less than 105 times in jail for various offences.[50]

This chapter will look at the types of crimes committed by Galway women in the late nineteenth century.

Drunkenness

Being drunk in a public place was a crime which carried a custodial sentence since 1861,[51] and rigorous statistics were submitted by the constabulary in each district showing the number of "habitual drunkards" in their region. In their report of 1876 the Inspectors General of Prisons in Ireland expressed concern that Irish jails were:

> chiefly occupied by prisoners of both sexes who are constantly recommitted for drunkenness, assaults and petty thefts, and by females of the depraved class, who have no honest means of livelihood.

The figures for Galway jail in 1875 showed that the number of female drunkards committed as "city or town prisoners" out-numbered males by ninety-four to ninety-two. This pattern is repeated in Dublin City, Cork City, Derry and Louth, but not in any of the rural prisons, suggesting that drunkenness amongst women was predominantly an urban problem.

In both 1881 and 1891, the majority of women sent to jail in Galway were imprisoned for being drunk, or drunk in conjunction with another crime, such as disorderly or obscene behaviour.

The police barracks at Eglinton Street, Galway, 1893

Many newspaper accounts of the Galway petty sessions in this period ended their reports with a reference to "the usual cases of drunkenness" which appeared before the magistrates. Intolerance of over-indulgence in alcohol was not the sole preserve of the police and politicians. The temperance movement, which had been led by Father Theobald Mathew in the mid-nineteenth century and carried on by Father Cullen in later years, was inextricably linked with the Catholic church. While the temperance movement and the "taking of the pledge" are more often associated with men than women in the nineteenth century, the evidence from prison records, judicial statistics and newspapers suggests that there was a notable public awareness of alcoholism amongst women. In 1881, the *Galway Vindicator* published a cautionary tale entitled:

The downward course of two beautiful women – drink.

One of these women, the newspaper informed its readers, had been "born in a castle" in Cork, and had recently been found by police in Erie with a gang of tramps "staggering from drink and weakness" and was destined to "spend her days in a workhouse".[52]

"Kate C.", who had formerly served a sentence of two months for neglecting her children, was arrested in 1891 for being drunk on the street and throwing stones through a shop window. She had had her two children with her when she committed the crime, one of them a baby, and the arresting constable stated in court that she was incapable of looking after them. The defendant told the magistrate:

I took the pledge on Saturday, and I will be able to look after them.[53]

Not all women were quite so penitent. "Mary B.", summoned for being drunk and disorderly in 1891, said in court that:

… she was no more drunk than at the present moment, and if the sergeant suspected she had anything taken now he was at liberty to smell her.

The sergeant testified that Mary's husband was a fisherman:

… and when he happened to be idle she was in the habit of beating him out of the house.

When the magistrate remarked that he never seen her in court before, she replied that:

COUNTY COURT HOUSE, GALWAY, with a View of the Bridge and County Gaol.

… about eleven years ago I was summoned by my brother-in-law, and about eight or nine years ago my sister-in-law had me up, and that does not speak bad for me.[54]

There were a number of women who were well known to the police and magistrates and who were obviously fond of "a drop". The following two cases appeared before the magistrates on the same day in June 1881, and were reported in the *Galway Express*:

Constable Pratt had a notorious bacchanalian named "Sally B." summoned for indulging in her usual propensity at the Claddagh, at about one o'clock on Sunday morning, the 22nd. inst. During her "little fit" she was not only noisy, the Constable stated, but when he arrived where she was performing, he observed her striking her fists in the air "boxing an imaginary foe". She was fined 1*s.* and costs.

"Kate C.", another of the same sisterhood, a real out-and-outer at sacrificing at the shrine of the rosy god, was sentenced to 14 days gaol exercise, for only being drunk two nights in succession during the past week, on each of which occasion she was kicking up "a dust" not agreeable to the neighbours who are so fortunate as to be located in the same alley as this black-eyed beauty. Owing to some cause or another she did not attend, whereupon a warrant was issued to enable her to be provided with a police escort to accompany her to her temporary destination.[55]

Judges arriving at the Galway Court-House for the Assizes.

Many cases of breaches of the licensing laws involved women who were publicans. "Mrs. Sarah B." was summoned in May 1891 for:

> ... admitting to her licensed premises a woman named "Ellen K." at 11.45 at night.[56]

At the petty sessions in October 1881, there were two cases involving women who were running shebeens, and one woman who was "found on".[57] In the following month, "Mrs. E. S." was fined one pound for selling intoxicating liquors with only a grocer's license, and "Bridget C." was fined ten pounds and costs for "keeping a shebeen house of low character" in Middle Street.[58]

Assault

The second most commonly found crime perpetrated by Galway women in 1881 and 1891 is assault. The local newspapers, particularly the *Galway Express*, reported many of these cases in great detail. Most of them appear to be the result of feuds between neighbours or family members, and many of them have cross-cases in which each party sues the other. One such case is that of a "… decent-looking woman" named "Mary M." who summoned an army pensioner called "Thomas M.", who, in turn summoned her. A witness in the case testified to having seen the woman spit in the face of the man, catch him by the neck, and saw her "coming out of a house and tearing off her shawl to fight" the pensioner.[59] Another report, entitled "How they live at the Small Crane", described a complicated cross-case of numerous assaults. The order of business in the court was as follows:

> "Biddy C." had "Kitty C." summoned for assault, "Mary C.", daughter to "Kitty", had "Nell C.", daughter to "Biddy", summoned for a similar offence, and "Biddy" had "Mary" summoned for abusive language, whilst "Andrew C.", husband to "Kitty", had "Biddy" summoned for abusive and threatening language.

According to Kate, a witness in this case, she had been drinking in Mr. Hardiman's public-house in Kitt's Corner. Biddy had offered to "treat" Kate to a pint, and had inadvertently knocked over Kitty's pint, whereupon a row ensued, in which Kitty:

> took the glass pint and flung it at Biddy … making her blood fly. She said she would be satisfied to give six months, as she saw Biddy's blood coming.[60]

It can be assumed that the "six months" refer to a prison sentence. She was sentenced to two weeks in jail and "taken into custody to enjoy the Christmas on prison diet".

A similar defiance was shown by many women in court, and the threat of a prison sentence was not a deterrent for some. When "Kate I." was summoned by her mother-in-law for assault in April 1891, she said that "she would go to jail before she'd give her mother-in-law that satisfaction".[61] In other cases, the assaults were of a more serious nature. An old woman called "Mary H." stabbed her landlady's daughter at her house in Market Street[62] in January 1891. The old woman, who admitted before the bench that she took a drop "to warm myself when I earn it honestly", had attempted to cut the throat of the younger woman.[63]

Assault cases between women attracted great attention from the press and public, as this extract from a report on an assault case in the *Galway Vindicator* in December 1891 shows:

> No matter what may be the circumstances attending combats between male pugilists their cases at the Petty Sessions court never attract the interest that one arising out of a female squabble does. When witnesses of the fair sex crowd the table there is generally a craning of necks on the part of the audience in the gallery and in the side seats to hear every word that is said … They gesticulate wildly, throw their shawl ends over their shoulders every second minute, and fling threatening words and looks at their opponents.[64]

Detailed and colourful descriptions of the appearance and comportment of the women involved were frequently included in the newspaper accounts. One of the women in the aforementioned case was Delia, who was described by the paper as being of "very prepossessing appearance". The article went on to say of her:

> … apparently, before entering the temple of justice, she had devoted some attention to the dressing of her hair; around her neck was a coloured necktie, and hanging on, and slipping off, her shoulders was what might be called a respectable shawl. A glance at her trembling fingers, through which she rolled two of those blue coloured documents known as summonses, showed that she was labouring under excitement.[65]

An interesting aspect of the assaults involving women is the number in which women were seen to play a prominent role in obstructing process-servers, bailiffs and police. At least seven of the assaults for which women were committed in 1881 involved attacks on police. In a case that came before the Connacht assizes in 1881, four men and four women were charged with riotous assembly and assault in Kilglass. A police Sub-Inspector gave evidence that, while protecting a process-server who was about to serve an eviction notice, they found women armed with sticks obstructing the doorways. A crowd of about four hundred gathered, and the police and process-servers were attacked with stones. According to the newspaper account of the evidence given, the women were the most vocal in the crowd, and one constable testified that:

> the women were throwing stones and mud, and the men were encouraging them and telling them that they were at their backs.[66]

In January of the same year, four women and a fourteen-year-old boy were indicted for unlawful assembly, and for assaulting a process-server near Clifden. The process-server suffered head injuries, including a fracture, and two witnesses testified to the fact that it was the women who were prominent in the crowd.[67] One of the most serious incidents of this kind occurred in Kiltimagh, when a crowd of about two hundred women attacked police attempting to serve a process. One woman was fatally wounded.[68] In October 1880, a forty-year-old woman was held in Galway jail for examination at the assizes for having thrown "a vessel with boiling water and lime into a bailiff's face".[69] Some sentences for riot, riotous assembly and riotous behaviour resulted from women's participation in mass protests at the scene of evictions.

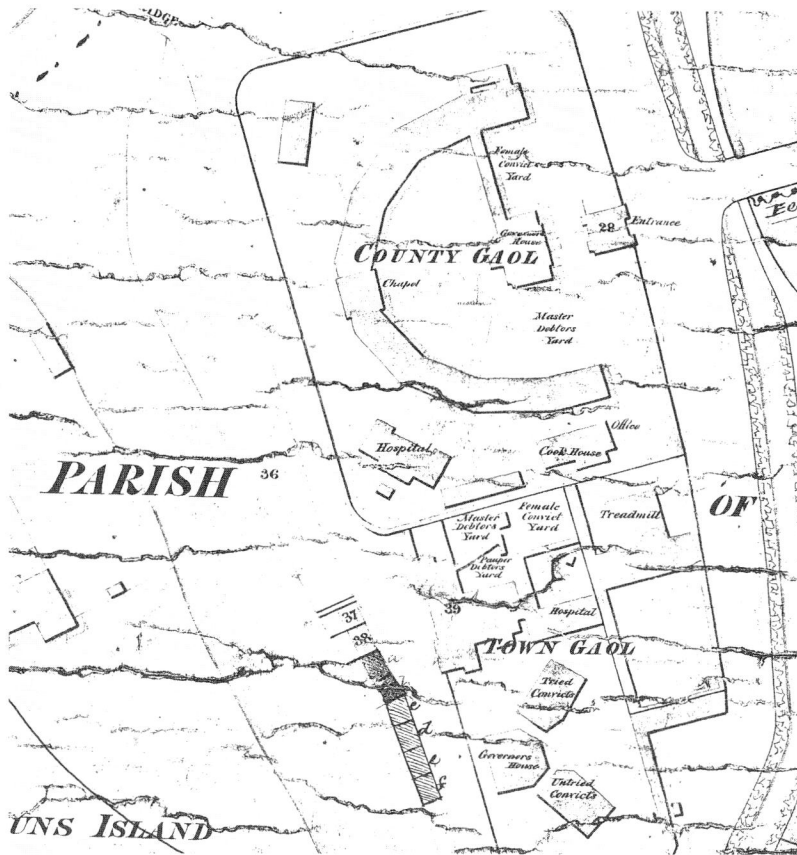

Griffith's Valuation Map of 1855,
showing the County and Town Jails.

Disorderly conduct

The prison registers do not always give the full details of the assault and riot charges, therefore it is difficult to ascertain the exact number of women who were involved in riots or assaults with the purpose of preventing evictions. "Riotous behaviour" also referred to disturbances caused by women on the streets, particularly when drunk or fighting. "Disorderly conduct", "obstruction" and "obscenity" also commonly referred to similar offences. Many of the women convicted of these crimes were hucksters or prostitutes, and much of their working lives was spent on the streets. They were frequently charged with a combination of offences, such as "disorderly conduct and obscene language". One woman, described by the newspaper as a "fowl huxter [sic]", appeared as both complainant and defendant in two related cases at the petty sessions on the same day in April 1891. In the first case, she summoned a local butcher for having assaulted her. She accused him of having had her evicted from her lodgings. According to her evidence, when he saw her after her eviction, he had said, "Thank God you are out of the place", and then gave her a "shove" and knocked her down. However, she was summoned for being drunk and disorderly on the same day by Constable Mullane. He testified that she wanted to beat the butcher:

> and when she failed in this, she vented her passion on the window shutters of a shop in Lombard-Street.[70]

The disorderly charge was sometimes entered as "disorderly on the public street" in the prison registers. Many of the women who were so charged were prostitutes, and this may have been a means of getting them off the streets. However, the existing records do not always give details of the circumstances of their crimes, and newspaper editors became increasingly reluctant to openly refer to prostitution in their papers as the nineteenth century progressed.

Prostitution

How a woman came to be officially described as a "prostitute" in the late nineteenth century is difficult to ascertain. The Dublin Police Act of 1842 stated that a woman known to a policeman as a prostitute and seen by him approaching men could be arrested. In Galway, however, only eight women were arrested for the crime of prostitution in 1881 and none in 1891. The crimes which were entered in the registers for these women were either "loitering for prostitution" or "importuning for purposes of prostitution". However, approximately sixteen per cent of women imprisoned in Galway in 1881 and 1891 had "prostitute" entered as their trade or occupation in the registers. The majority of those who did end up in the jail were arrested for a range of crimes such as drunkenness, disorderly behaviour, obscenity or theft.

Most of the prostitutes who were sentenced would appear, from the available evidence, to have worked the streets, and much of their clientele was drawn from the ranks of the soldiers and sailors who frequented the town. It is sometimes difficult to establish from the newspaper accounts and the prison registers whether a woman was a prostitute or not. For example, in January 1881, three young women from the "classic region" of Shell Lane in the west of the city were arrested for causing an obstruction. The arresting officer testified that "those angelic creatures", as the newspaper described them, were found "flag-dancing" in William Street West. He further gave evidence that:

they were in the habit of making a practice of inviting all soldiers and sailors passing by to join in the merry dance, but did not pay any attention to the police force other than to make themselves scarce.[71]

These girls, who were aged between fifteen and seventeen years, were not listed as prostitutes in any of their many appearances in the prison registers. Another woman, "Biddy B.", a witness in an assault case, and a woman who served a number of custodial sentences in Galway, was described in the newspaper as:

a kind-hearted nymph of nocturnal propensities.[72]

Her occupation in the prison register was "factory-girl".

There were a number of women who made frequent appearances in the courts and prison and were well known to the police and magistrates. These women would have been what the General Prisons Board members would have referred to in their reports as "incorrigible females". They were prostitutes, probably alcoholic, or at least regular drinkers, and frequently homeless. Some of them moved from town to town, and it is, therefore, difficult to follow their movements. It is unlikely that many of these women lived to old age, given the hardships they encountered. However, the 1901 census reveals that there were four known prostitutes in the Galway workhouse on census night. One was aged sixty, and another seventy.

Many prostitutes would appear to have used the workhouse for shelter, and, it has been suggested, for soliciting. At a meeting of the Galway Union in 1881, a

Guardian who was trying to gain admission to the workhouse for a sick old man said that:

> it was unfair that a man such as this applicant should be refused admission when "strumpets" of girls who should not be allowed in were never refused.[73]

The courts often looked more favourably on prostitutes or women of "bad character" who were willing to go to the Magdalen asylum. Two women, "Eliza E." and "Mary Ellen H.", were arrested on separate charges of larceny in the same week in October 1881. Both appear in the prison register as "prostitutes". Eliza had left the Asylum after three years and was found by police in the company of "some of the worst characters in Galway". She attempted to rob a seaman with whom she was walking on Shop Street late at night. Mary Ellen had escaped from the Magdalen Asylum by scaling the walls and had stolen from it a pair of petticoats, a jacket, an apron, a pair of boots and a pair of stockings. Mary Ellen was described by the newspaper as being about seventeen years of age, with "a beautiful cast of countenance". She claimed in court that when she had tried to go back with the clothes, the Asylum had refused to take her. The magistrate in both cases told the prisoners that he would deal leniently with them if they agreed to go back to the Asylum. Eliza, who was:

> respectably dressed, and apparently very much ashamed of her conduct…

promised to go back to the Magdalen and was sentenced to a month's hard labour. Mary Ellen refused to go back, and, according to the newspaper account of her trial, stamped her

THE STATE OF IRELAND: SCENE OUTSIDE THE COURTHOUSE, GALWAY.—SEE PAGE 154.
FROM A SKETCH BY OUR SPECIAL ARTIST.

foot and told the magistrate "No I will never go back there". She was sentenced to three months hard labour.[74] While both were charged with similar crimes, their treatment at the hands of the magistrates was very different, and sentencing appears to have been rather arbitrarily based on the degree of penitence shown in each case.

Part of the difficulty in identifying who was or was not a prostitute arises from the fact that, in the last decades of the nineteenth century, a combination of Victorian modesty and the sober influence of the Catholic Church made open discussion of sex and related issues virtually non-existent. Reporting of crimes involving prostitution changed dramatically from the mid- to the late-nineteenth century. While the official records, such as the prison registers, record the term "prostitute" as a trade or occupation, one has to carefully read between the lines of the newspaper accounts for synonyms such as "nymphs", "ladies of the pave" and "Cyprians".[75]

Other crimes

In 1881 and 1891, child-related offences formed approx-imately four to ten percent of the crimes of women in Galway. This category includes "concealment of birth", "exposing children" (to danger or unnecessary suffering), abandoning children and infanticide. It is not always clear from the records whether the babies involved in the "concealment" cases survived, and some "concealment" cases may have involved infanticide. In 1891, two women,

"Honoria H.", aged twenty, and "Mary H.", aged sixty, were imprisoned on a concealment charge. It is probable that Mary was Honoria's mother or aunt. Mary was sentenced to one month's hard labour, and Honoria was remanded to the assizes and subsequently transferred to Limerick prison. Since Honoria was transferred to a convict prison to serve out a long sentence, it is probable that the baby died as a result of the concealment.[76] In the prison registers, these offences were also written in as "menacing her newly-born child", "suspicion of murdering her newly-born infant" and, in the case of one eighteen-year-old girl, "attempting to choke her infant child". The sentences were not always unduly harsh. One woman of thirty who was convicted of "murdering her illegitimate child" in 1880, was sentenced to five calendar months in jail.[77] The *Galway Vindicator* carried a brief report in December 1881 on the trial of a girl of sixteen from Eyrecourt who "wept bitterly" while being charged with endeavouring to conceal the birth of her child.[78] She was sentenced to six weeks in jail. A twenty-year-old servant was acquitted of the charge of murdering her child in May 1890. In May of the following year, a young woman was tried for the murder of a baby boy whose body was found in Ballybane:

> … concealed between two rocks, and covered over with small stones …

According to the newspaper, the woman:

> sat quite unconcerned during the taking down of the evidence.

A number of witnesses testified to having known the girl, none of whom showed any sympathy towards her or understanding of her situation. A woman who had worked with her as a servant in Tuam, and shared a bed with her in her employer's house, told her mistress that she:

> could not be in the house with them because she was in the family way.[79]

Attempted suicide was an offence for which a person could be sent to jail, and there were some women who were imprisoned more than once for this "crime". Of the two women who were imprisoned for attempting suicide in a two-year period (1890–91), both were prostitutes. The reports of the Inspectors of the prisons show that other prisoners attempted to kill themselves after they had been sent to prison. One local newspaper, in its account of the proceedings at the Quarter Sessions in October 1891, reported that there were only two criminal cases for trial, one an assault, and:

> the other was a silly creature who attempted suicide.[80]

Despite the poverty which existed in Galway in the late nineteenth century, theft and larceny were less common than one might expect. Most of the thefts in both 1881 and 1891 were of items of clothing, but money, food, hay, turf, fowl and even grass were stolen. Perhaps the most unusual item to be recorded as stolen in the prison registers involved the case of a woman and her female child who were sent to jail for a month in 1899 for "larceny of a quantity of hair".

Many of the crimes for which people were sent to jail in the last century appear somewhat baffling to us today. In September 1880, a factory-girl was sentenced to forty-eight hours in jail for causing an obstruction by dancing on the street. In April 1881, a forty-year-old prostitute was sentenced to a month's hard labour for "being found sleeping in the open air". This, like begging, was a criminal offence under the Vagrancy Acts. Whether the seeming harshness of this sentence masked a desire on the part of the magistrate to provide shelter for this woman, or an intolerance of such an immoral woman sleeping in a public place, we shall probably never know.

The back door of Galway jail.

"Maggie M."

Age: 43
Crime: larceny

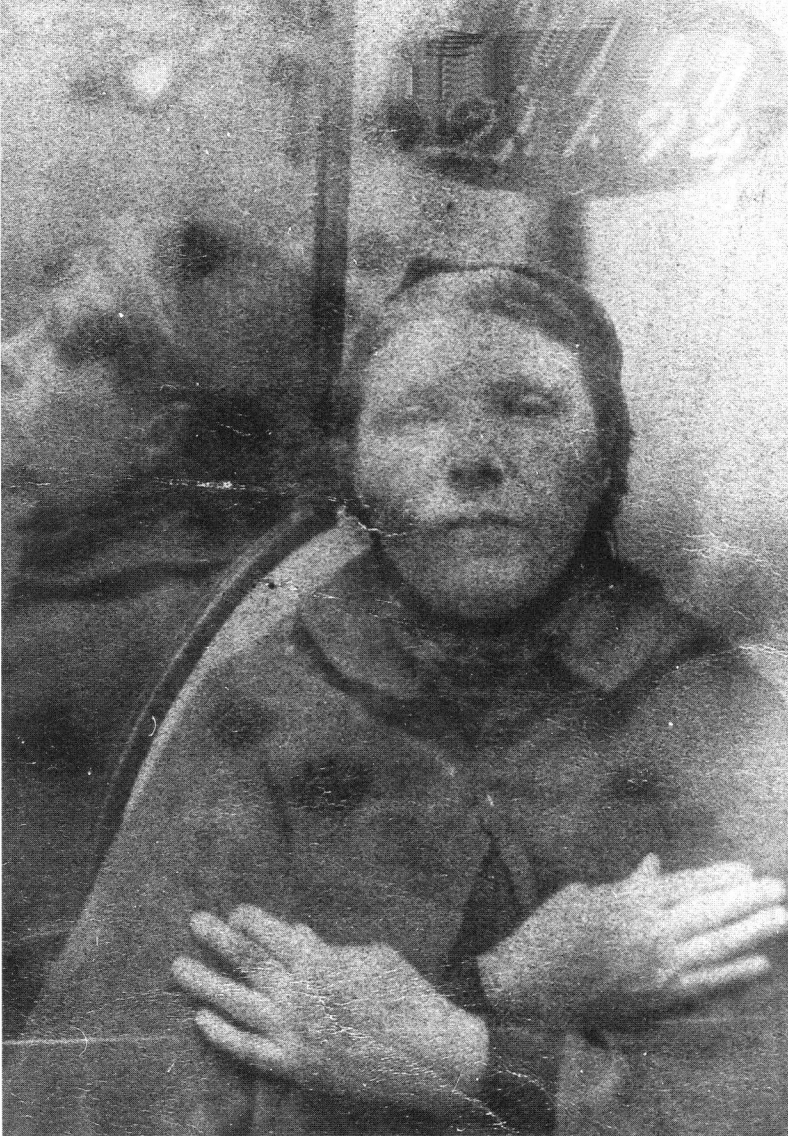

Maggie was sentenced to three years in Grangegorman in 1892 for larceny. The records state that she:

is a prostitute, has four previous convictions for larceny recorded against her and one hundred and twelve convictions for petty offences.

The Governor of Galway jail wrote that:

She was known in this town for over 20 years to be a prostitute of the lowest type. She, however, apparently reformed in 1888 and kept out of prison for three years, during which time she lived by the sale of fruit, which she hawked in a basket. In 1891, she was arrested for the illegal possession of a watch, which was alleged she stole from a man, in whose company she was thought to be for immoral purposes. The constabulary are under the impression that since that time she has relapsed into her former habits of immorality and that she is now, what she was then – a prostitute.

Photograph, with statement in reference to final disposal.

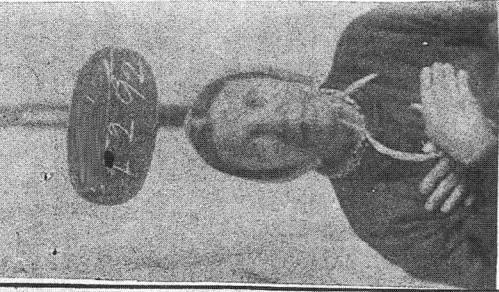

Released from H.M. Prison Grangegorman on Licence of $\frac{361}{365}$ yr. on the 26th January /94 and sent to Galway

E.J. McCarthy
Superintendent
27.1.94

Convicted at Galway P. Sess. on 12.8.95 of Riotous and Indecent behaviour, & sentenced to 14 dys. N.L. or 21/6.?

Convicted on 16.9.95 at Galway P. Sess of obscene language, sentenced to 14 dys. N.L. or 21/6: (committed 5.10.95): licence expired on 22.10.95; no action taken.

(11922/75)

A Galway R.I.C. Inspector wrote of Maggie:

> Through the influence of the clergy she was fairly reformed …
> but about a year ago she again took to drink and returned to
> her former life of prostitution, but not so openly as the other
> common prostitutes of the town and with whom she did not
> associate.

While in Grangegorman, Maggie sent two letters, and received none.

Prior to her release, she asked for ten shillings to be given to her on discharge, to help her to buy fruit and vegetables for sale.

In 1899, Maggie served two sentences, one for riotous and indecent behaviour, and another for begging and obscene language.

Conclusion

Late nineteenth century Galway was a county of high emigration, particularly amongst women, and of high unemployment for those who stayed behind. While educational opportunities and standards were improving, they were not keeping pace with the rest of the country. There were very few options for poor women, other than assisted emigration or the workhouse. Many lived very close to, or below, the poverty line, and it is from this socio-economic group that the majority of women who became involved in crime was drawn.

Most of women sentenced to jail in Galway in 1881 and 1891 were in their thirties, illiterate and unskilled. The majority, however, had a trade or occupation of some kind, and there are no women in the 1891 register whose trade is listed as "nil". The crimes of which they were found guilty were predominantly alcohol-related, and there is some evidence to suggest that at certain times during the late nineteenth century women in Galway were more likely than men to be arrested for this type of crime. Many Galway women were litigious, and local feuds often developed into violence and ended in the courts. Others were found guilty of "protest" or "agrarian" crimes and often showed a greater propensity for violent action than their menfolk when protecting their homes. The types of crime perpetrated by Galway women in this period, and their sometimes defiant and hostile behaviour on the streets and in the courts, displayed a strong deviation from the prevalent and somewhat aspirational Victorian image of the "gentle" sex.

As the century progressed, the numbers of women involved in crime fell dramatically. Of the twenty-three women in Galway jail on the night of 1 April 1901, only four were under the age of thirty. While this fall in criminal activity is certainly related to the decrease in population, particularly in the west, there were other factors which influenced the change. By 1901, criminal women in the west of Ireland lived in a society where they had become increasingly marginalized. Sexual morality, drunkenness and deviation from the perceived norms of respectability and accepted behaviour had become public issues. The Victorian passion for law and order meant that drunkenness, begging, and even dancing on the street were crimes. Those who were considered "lunatic" were sent to asylums and drunkards were sent to reformatories under the new Inebriates Act of 1898. The Catholic Church was placing increased emphasis on sobriety and chastity. Women were "simultaneously idealized and repressed".[81] Prostitutes and other "wayward" girls were sent to Magdalen asylums. Meanwhile, educational standards were raised and opportunities for employment were slowly improving. The women who populated Galway jail in the late nineteenth century in many ways represented a past that Ireland wanted to leave behind.

EPILOGUE

Galway jail was closed in 1939, and ownership of the property was transferred from the Department of Justice to the county council. In 1941, the council handed over the site to the Catholic diocese of Galway, Kilmacduagh and Kilfenora. It was decided by the bishop and the diocesan trustees that this would be an appropriate place to build a new cathedral. The jail was sold for a nominal sum of 10 pounds, and the keys were handed over to the bishop by the council in 1941. In the same year, the jail buildings were demolished, and only the surrounding walls were left standing.

Construction of the cathedral began in 1958, and it was completed in 1965. The only clue which remains to indicate that a prison stood on the site is a memorial which is dedicated to the executed prisoners of Galway jail.

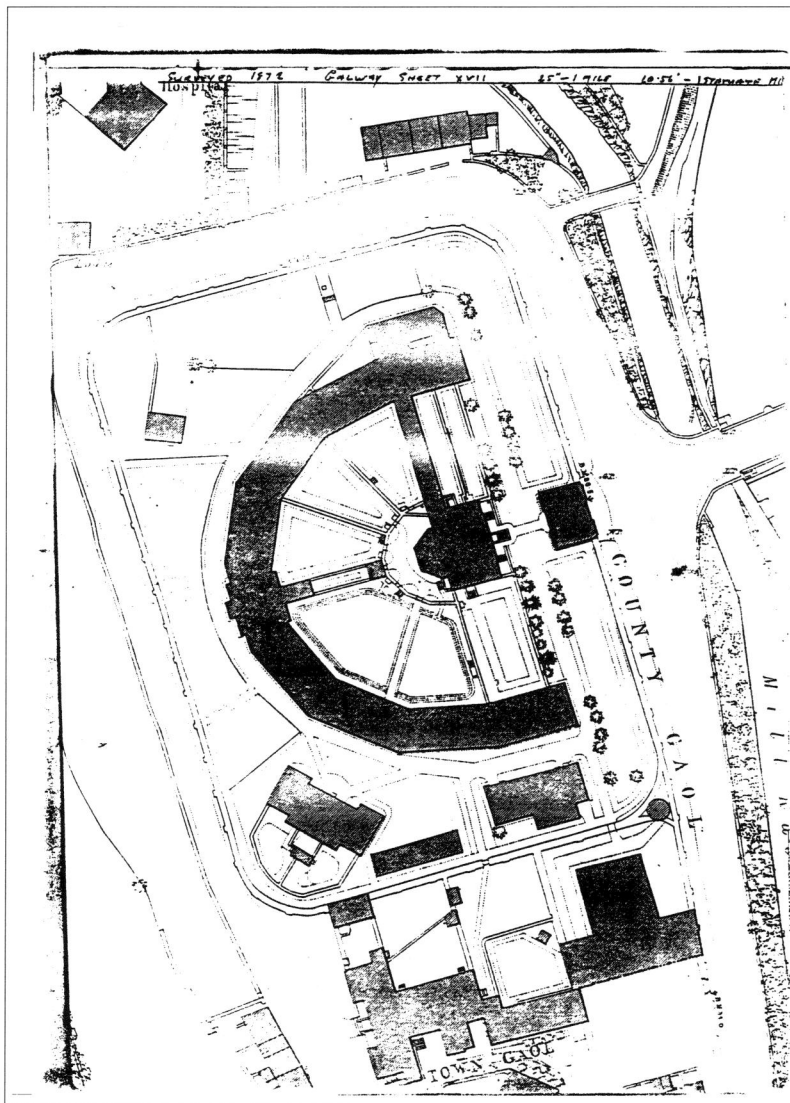

Ordnance Survey map of 1872.

PRISON PASSES

MEMORIES OF GALWAY JAIL

With the closing of Galway Jail on Monday, Connacht has now only one prison—Sligo—although each of the five counties had one not so long ago. All the bridewells in the province have also been closed.

Persons who ordinarily would be sent to Galway Prison, will in future, it is stated, be accommodated in Limerick or Sligo.

How the prison is to be used in future has not been decided. Apart from the prison building itself, there are also dwellings outside built by the General Prisons Board.

Described by F. J. Higginbotham, in his book, "The Vivid Life; a Journalist's Career," as " a black and forbidding pile of granite on the banks of the River Corrib," the prison contains the bones of men whom many people in the West still believe were wrongly executed.

One of these was Myles Joyce, who, with two others, was hanged there on December 15, 1882, for the " Maamtrasna murders" in North Connemara. Joyce on the scaffold made in Irish a statement protesting his innocence, and forgiving those who had sworn his life away.

The statement, which was saved for posterity by an Irish-speaking reporter, had a profound effect. The condemned man said:—

" Nil me cionntach. Ni raibh lamh no cos agam ins an marbhadh. Ni feasach me nidh ar bith ina thimcheall. Go maithidh Dia don mhuintir a mbionnuigh in m'aghaidh. Go bhfoire Dia ar mo bhean agus ar a cuigear dileachta. Ach ta mo shagart liom. Taim chomh neamhchionntach leis an leanbh ata sa gcliabhan."

Another man executed there and whom large numbers believed was innocent was Patrick Walsh, convicted of the " Letterfrack murders " in Connemara.

The *Connacht Tribune*,
May 6 1939.

WHERE GALWAY'S NEW CATHEDRAL WILL RISE

His Lordship, the Most Rev. Dr. Browne, Bishop of Galway, on Wednesday week received from Mr. Eamon Corbett, chairman of the Galway Co. Council, the keys of the Galway County Jail, on the site of which the Lord Bishop proposes to erect a Cathedral. In the group are (left to right): His Worship the Mayor, Ald. J. F. Costello, P.C., H.C.; the Very Rev. P. Glynn, Adm., St. Nicholas's N. and E.; the Bishop of Galway; Mr. E. Corbett, Mr. Martin Quinn, chairman of the County Council's Finance Committee; the Very Rev. P. Canon Davis, P.P., Rahoon; Mr. C. I. O'Flynn, Co. Commissioner, and Mr. G. Lee, B.E., County Surveyor.   [TRIBUNE Photo.

In a letter to Galway county council, Bishop Browne wrote;

> I am advised that the jail site would make a most suitable emplacement for a cathedral; it is spacious with dignified and beautiful surroundings, not hemmed in with unsightly buildings, but with magnificent approaches and views on each side. Forty years ago my predecessors could not have dreamed that this site would become available for a cathedral. Today, under native Irish Government, a jail is not required in Co. Galway…Now that the site has become available I submit to you that there could be no more noble or more fitting use than to erect on it a cathedral in thanksgiving to God Who sustained our people in their days of trial.

Aerial photograph which shows the Courthouse,
the Salmon Weir Bridge (formerly called the "Gaol Bridge"),
and the jail, prior to demolition.

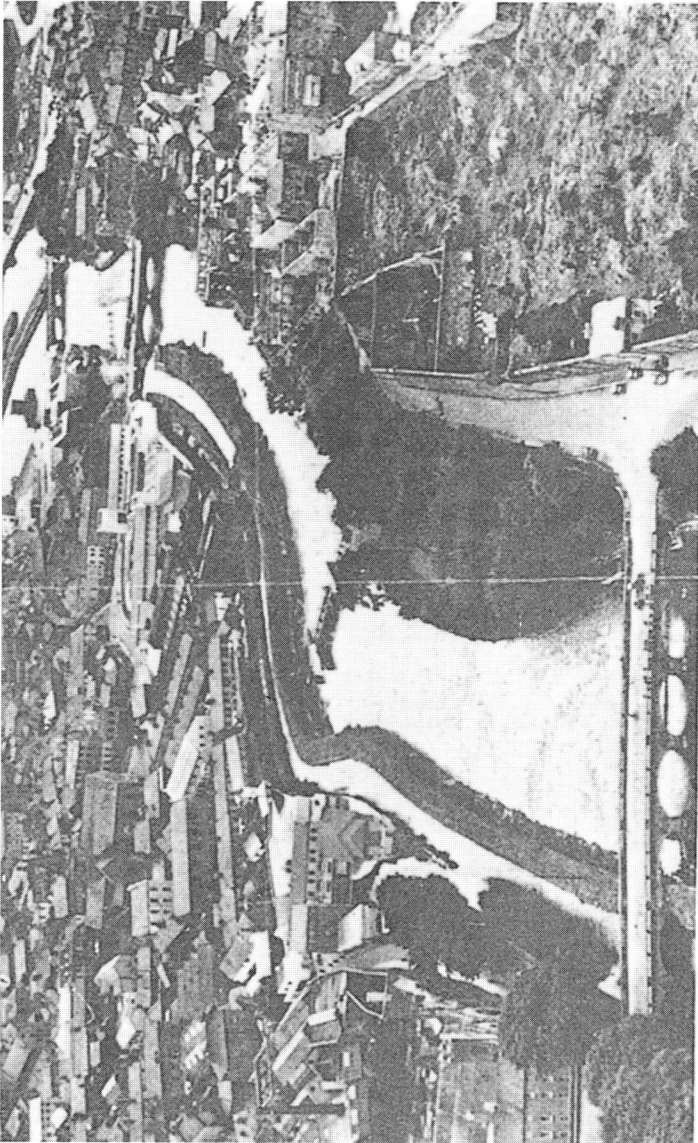

Aerial photograph, with the site of the jail in the foreground, on the right. Only the walls remain standing.

NOTES

1 *First report of the General Prisons Board (hereafter GPB),* 1878–79, H.C.XXXIV.353, Appendix, p. 41.

2 *Census of Ireland 1901,* Part I, Vol. IV.

3 J. H. Tuke, "With the emigrants", in *The nineteenth century,* Vol.XII, 1882.

4 *Census of Ireland 1891,* General Report Part II.

5 *Census of Ireland 1901,* Part I, Vol. IV.

6 *Census of Ireland 1881,* Part II.

7 *Census of Ireland 1891,* Part II.

8 *Census of Ireland 1901,* Part I, Vol. IV.

9 *Census of Ireland 1891,* General Report, Part II.

10 *Census of Ireland 1871,* Part I, Vol. IV.

11 *Census of Ireland 1901,* Part I, Vol. IV. A change in classification of occupations occurred after 1871, which may, in part, account for this decrease.

12 *Thom's Official Directory* 1881 (Dublin 1881)

13 *Ibid.*

14 *Return of inmates of workhouses (Ireland),* Feb. 1883, 1884, LXVIII.61

15 *Ibid.*

16 *Return of mortality of children in Irish workhouses 1881,* 1882, LIX.97.

17 See, for example, David Fitzpatrick, "'A Share of the Honeycomb': Education, emigration and Irishwomen", in

Mary Daly and David Dickson (eds), *The origins of popular literacy in Ireland: Language change and educational development 1700–1920* (Dublin 1990).

18 *The Galway Express,* August 27 1881.

19 *Ibid.* April 25 1891.

20 *Ibid.* August 27 1881.

21 *Ibid.* August 20 1881.

22 *Criminal and judicial statistics, Ireland (1871),* {C.674}, H.C. 1872, LVX.235, 31.

23 E. OE. Somerville and V. M. Ross, *Through Connemara in a governess cart, with a new introduction by William Trevor* (London 1893).

24 Lady Gregory, *The gaol gate,* Dublin 1918.

25 *Report of the general state of prisons of Ireland 1818,* H.C. 1819, (534) XII. 453.

26 *Ninth report on the general state of prisons in Ireland 1830–31,* (172) IV. 269.

27 *Ibid.*

28 *Eighteenth report on the general state of prisons in Ireland 1840,* [240] XXVI.165.

29 The treadwheel was a form of prison labour usually reserved for able-bodied male prisoners. The inspectors' report of 1850 stated that in the Galway jails "… it turns a mill which grinds a sufficient quantity of meal for the use of the prison; it has a small tuck-mill attached to it, which answers for scouring blankets, frieze … and a machine for grinding bones also". The treadwheel in Galway jail was demolished in 1883.

30 *Twenty-eighth report on the general state of prisons in Ireland 1850,* [1229] XXIX.305.

31 *Thirty-eighth report on the general state of prisons in Ireland 1860,* [2691] XXXVI.191.

32 An increase in the number of male prisoners resulted from the Better Protection of Persons and Property Act of 1881, and the imprisonment of those involved in protest and agrarian crimes in general also led to a significant increase

in committals in the early 1880's. Warders from Mountjoy prison were brought to local prisons to supplement existing staff levels as a result.

33 1859 Session 1 (17) 1.331.

34 *Fourteenth report of the GPB* 1892 [C.6789] XLII.245.

35 Wilfrid Scawen Blunt, *My diaries, being a personal narrative of events, 1881–1914, Part Two* (London 1920).

36 Lucia Zedner, *Women, crime and custody in Victorian England* (Oxford, 1994).

37 Peter Broderick's *Prison Diary, 1881–82* (Privately held – a copy is also held in the James Hardiman Library, NUI, Galway).

38 Coir is a rough fibre used in the making of mats and ropes, and oakum-picking involved the loosening of the strands of old ropes. Wilfrid Scawen Blunt, in his account of his time in Galway jail, described how "… the oakum picking was so little a trouble to me that I came to be glad to secrete a piece of the tarred rope on Saturday nights so as to have it to pick on Sundays".

39 It is possible to identify prisoner "A.O." with reasonable certainty from other appearances in the records. A woman with the same initials and fitting her description appeared in the jail register in 1881, having been sentenced for a range of crimes including drunkenness, breaking windows, profane language, prostitution, stabbing, attempted suicide and riotous and disorderly behaviour. On one occasion, she was arrested for drunkenness with her husband.

40 The fourteenth report of the inspectors noted that "In Galway there had been a number of cases of typhoid fever in the town, in the neighbourhood of the prison, before the disease appeared in the prison itself. During the autumn there had been an unusual drought, and the level of the river had fallen unprecedentedly low, so that not only did the general water supply fail, but the neighbourhood of the river, close to which the prison is situated, became occasionally very offensive".

41 *Fourteenth report of the GPB 1892* [C.6789] XLII.245.

42 *Seventh report of the GPB 1884–85* [C.4543] XXXVIII.783.

43 *Eighth report of the GPB 1886* [C.4817] XXXV.281.

44 *Ibid.*

45 *Fourteenth report of the GPB 1892* [C.6789] XLII.245.

46 C. Lombroso and W. Ferrero, *The Female Offender* (London, 1959, originally published London, 1895).

47 *The Galway Vindicator and Connaught Advertiser* (hereafter the *Galway Vindicator*) 23 February 1891.

48 Recidivism amongst women is a recurring theme in contemporary parliamentary papers and studies of crime. The government inspector who visited the Galway jails in 1871 found fifty males and sixty-nine females committed for drunkenness on the day of his visit. He stated that "… it is a disgrace to the district that the number of female commitments of drunkards should exceed that of males". Referring to the crime statistics for 1869 and 1870, he goes on to report that "Four times was the utmost that any male was committed in either year, whereas females were committed in both years as often as fifteen times". (Forty-ninth report of the Inspectors General of Prisons, 1871 [C.359], XXX.1).

49 *Appendix to fifty-fourth rep. separate reps. on county and city gaols and bridewells*, 1876 {C.1497–1} XXXVI.77.

50 *The Galway Express*, 10th September 1881.

51 Bill to enable justices in Ireland to commit to local bridewells persons convicted of drunkenness, 1861 (218), II.145.

52 *The Galway Vindicator*, 7th September 1881.

53 *The Galway Express*, 31st January 1891.

54 *Ibid*, 24th January 1891.

55 *Ibid*, 4th June 1881.

56 *Ibid*, 16th May 1891.

57 *The Galway Vindicator*, 19th October 1881.

58 *Ibid*, 9th November 1881.

59 *The Galway Express,* 27th June 1891.

60 *Ibid.,* 17th December 1881.

61 *Ibid.,* 18th April 1891.

62 The *Express* reported this crime as having happened at a house in Market Street, whereas the *Vindicator* reported that it happened in Middle Street.

63 *The Galway Express,* 17th January 1891.

64 *The Galway Vindicator,* 9th December 1891.

65 *Ibid.*

66 *Ibid.,* 10th December 1881.

67 *The Galway Express,* 29th January 1881.

68 *Ibid.,* 9th. April 1881.

69 General Register, Galway gaol, 1880-85 (National Archives 1/21/12).

70 *The Galway Express,* April 18th 1891.

71 *Ibid.,* 8th January 1881.

72 *Ibid.,* 19th March 1881.

73 *Ibid.,* 14th May 1881.

74 *Ibid.,* 29th October 1881.

75 See Ciaran O Murchadha, "Paphian nymphs and worshippers of the Idalian goddess: Prostitution in Ennis in the mid-nineteenth century" in *The Other Clare,* Vol. 24 (2000), and also Ronald Pearsall, *The worm in the bud; the world of Victorian sexuality,* (Harmondsworth 1971).

76 General register, Galway gaol 1886–92, (National Archives 1/21/13).

77 General Register, Galway gaol, 1880–5 (National Archives 1/21/12).

78 *The Galway Vindicator,* 17th December 1881.

79 *The Galway Express,* 9th, 23rd, and 30th May 1891.

80 *The Galway Vindicator,* 24th October 1891.

81 Joseph J. Lee, "Women and the church since the Famine" in Margaret MacCurtain and Donnchadh O Corrain (eds.) *Women in Irish Society: the Historical Dimension* (Dublin 1978), pp. 37–45.

BIBLIOGRAPHY

Manuscript sources

Correspondence register of the General Prisons Board (G.P.B./C.R./73).

Penal Record Files 1882–95.

Prison register, Galway jail – general register 1858–1875 (1/21/6).

— 1865–1875 (1/21/7).

— 1876–1878 (1/21/10).

— 1878–1880 (1/21/11).

— 1880–1885 (1/21/12).

— 1886–1892 (1/21/13).
— 1892–1899 (1/21/14).

— index, general 1888–1894 (1/21/21).

— 1894–1898 (1/21/22).

— *All held at the National Archives, Dublin*

Peter Broderick's prison diary, 1881–2 (Privately held. A copy is also held in the James Hardiman Library, NUI, Galway).

Parliamentary papers

Inspectors general report on the general state of prisons of Ireland, 1818, 1819 (534) XII.453.

— Ninth report, 1830–31 [172] IV.269.

— Eighteenth report, 140 [240] XXVI.165.

— Twenty-eighth report, 1850 [1229] XXIX.305.

— Thirty-eighth report, 1860 [2691] XXXVI.191.

— Thirty-ninth report, 1861 [2861] XXIX.181.

— Forty-ninth report, 1871 [C.359] XXX.I.

— Fiftieth report, 1872 [C.535] XXXII.1.

— Fifty-sixth report, 1878 [C.2160] XLII.107.

— Appendix to fifty-fourth report, separate reps. on county and city gaols and bridewells 1876 {C.1497–1} XXXVI.77.

General prisons board (Ireland):

— First report, 1878 1878–79 [C.2447] XXXIV.353.

— Second report, 1879–80 1880 [C.2689] XXXV.211.

— Third report, 1880–81 1881 [C.3067] LI.665.

— Fourth report, 1881–82 1882 [C.3360] XXXIII.661.

— Fifth report, 1882–83 1883 [C.3757] XXXII.811.

— Sixth report, 1883–84 1884 [C.4158] XLII.705.

— Seventh report, 1884–85 1884–85 [C.4543] XXXVIII.783.

— Eighth report, 1885–86 1886 [C.4817] XXXV.281.

— Ninth report, 1886–87 1887 [C.5224] XLI.535.

— Tenth report, 1887–88 1888 [C.5547] LVIII.391.

— Eleventh report, 1888–89 1889 [C.5816] XLI.497.

— Twelfth report, 1889–90 1890 [C.6182] XXXVII.291.

— Thirteenth report, 1890–91 1890-91 [C.6451] XLIII.227.

— Fourteenth report, 1891–92 1892 [C.6789] XLII.245.

— Fifteenth report, 1892–93 1893-94 [C.7174] XLVII.219.

— Sixteenth report, 1893–94 1894 [C.7560] XLIV.279.

— Seventeenth report, 1894–95 1895 [C.7806] LVI.967.

— Eighteenth report, 1895–96 1896 [C.8252] XLIV.679.

— Nineteenth report, 1896–97 1897 [C.8589] XL.545.

— Twentieth report, 1897–98 1898 [C.8930] XLVII.513.

— Twenty-first report, 1898–99 1899 [C.9439] XLIII.585.

— Twenty-second report, 1899–1900 1900 [Cd.293] XLI.577.
Criminal and judicial statistics of Ireland 1871 1872 {C.674}
LVX.235.

— 1881 1882 {C.3355} LXXV.243.

— 1891 1892 {C.7189}CIII.279.

Census of Ireland

— 1871, Vol.IV, Part I, No.1.

— 1881, General report, Part II .

— 1891, General report, part II.

— 1901, Vol.IV, Part I, No.1 (County of Galway).

— 1901, returns for District Electoral Division, Galway West Urban.

Bill for consolidating and amending laws relating to county prisons in Ireland, 1859 Session 1 (17), I.331.

Bill to enable justices in Ireland to commit to local bridewells persons convicted of Drunkenness 1861 (218) II.145.

Bill to amend laws relating to prisons in Ireland 1877 V.107.

Bill for better protection of persons and property in Ireland, 1881 V.17, 44 Vic., Cap. 4.

Inebriates Act 1898 (122) LXXIX.565.

Royal Commission on administration, discipline and condition of prisons in Ireland, Preliminary report, 1883 [C.3496] XXXII.803.

Forty-sixth report of the Commissioners of national education in Ireland 1880 [C.2592] XXIII.57.

Report, Aug. 1880, from Captain D. Morant, Senior Naval Officer at Galway, in Reference to relief of distressed population on w. coast of Ireland 1880 [C.2671] LXII.195.

Statement by five Catholic bishops of west of Ireland relating to distress in Ireland, Jan. 1883 1883 LIX.49.

Mr. Tuke's report on relief of distress in west of Ireland (931-Sess.2) 1886 LVII.63.

Report on failure of potato crop and condition of poorer classes in w. of Ireland 1890–91 1890–91 LXIII.803.

Return of mortality of children in Irish workhouses 1881, 1882 LIX.97.

Return of inmates of workhouses (Ireland), Feb. 1883, 1884 LXVIII.61.

Newspapers and directories

The Galway Express 1875–1900.

The Galway Vindicator and Connaught Advertiser 1875–1900.

Thom's Official Directory 1881 (Dublin 1881).

Thom's Official Directory 1891 (Dublin 1891).

Books

Barnes, Jane. *Irish industrial schools, 1868–1908.* Dublin, 1989.

Blunt, Wilfrid Scawen. *My diaries, being a personal narrative of events, 1884–1914, part two.* London, 1920.

Byrne, Anne and Leonard, Madeleine (eds.). *Women and Irish society: A sociological Reader*. Belfast, 1997.

Carpenter, J. Estlin. *The life and work of Mary Carpenter*. London, 1879.

Coulter, Henry. *The west of Ireland: Its existing conditions and prospects*. Dublin, 1862.

Crossman, Virginia. *Local government in nineteenth-century Ireland*. Belfast, 1994.

Crossman, Virginia. *Politics, law and order in nineteenth-century Ireland*. Dublin, 1996.

Daly, Mary and Dickson, David (eds.). *The origins of popular literacy in Ireland: Language change and educational development*. Dublin, 1990.

Damousi, Joy. *Depraved and disorderly: Female convicts, sexuality and gender in Colonial Australia*. Cambridge, 1997.

Diner, Hasia R. *Erin's daughters in America; Irish immigrant women in the nineteenth Century*. Baltimore 1983.

Englander, David. *Poverty and poor law reform in Britain: From Chadwick to Booth, 1834–1914*. London, 1998.

Finnegan, Frances. *Poverty and prostitution; a study of Victorian prostitutes in York*, Cambridge, 1979

Foucault, Michel. *Discipline and punish. The birth of the prison*. Trans. New York, 1979.

Hahn Rafter, Nicole. *Partial Justice; Women in state prisons 1800–1935*. Boston, 1985.

Hahn Rafter, Nicole. White trash. *The Eugenic family studies 1877–1919*. Boston, 1988.

Hardiman, James. *History of the town and county of the town of Galway*. Dublin, 1820.

Heidensohn, Frances. *Women and crime*. London, 1985.

Huntsman, Richard. *Elizabeth Fry, 1780–1845*. London, 1998.

Ignatieff, Michael. *A just measure of pain: the penitentiary in the industrial revolution 1750–1850*. New York, 1978.

Jones, Greta and Malcolm, Elizabeth. *Medicine, disease and the state in Ireland, 1650–1940*. Cork, 1999.

Kelleher, Margaret and Murphy, James H. *Gender perspectives in nineteenth–century Ireland: Public and private spheres*. Dublin, 1997.

Kent, John. *Elizabeth Fry*. London, 1962.

Kerrigan, Colm. *Fr. Mathew and the Irish temperance movement: 1838–1849*. Cork, 1992.

Langan–Egan, Maureen. *Galway women in the nineteenth century*. Dublin, 1999.

Lombroso, C. and Ferrero, W. *The female offender*. London, 1959, (originally published London 1895).

Luddy, Maria and Murphy, Cliona (eds.). *Women Surviving*. Dublin, 1990.

Luddy, Maria. *Women and philanthropy in nineteenth-century Ireland*. Cambridge, 1995.

Luddy, Maria. *Women in Ireland, 1800–1918: A documentary history.* Cork, 1995.

MacCurtain, Margaret and O'Corrain, Donnchadh. *Women in Irish society: The historical dimension.* Dublin, 1978.

Malcolm, Elizabeth. *'Ireland sober, Ireland free'; drink and temperance in nineteenth-century Ireland.* Dublin, 1986

Mayhew, Henry. *The criminal prisons of London and scenes of prison life.* London, 1862.

Moran, Gerard (ed.). *Galway history and society: Inter-disciplinary essays on the history of an Irish county.* Dublin, 1996.

Morris, Norval and Rothman, David J. (eds.). *The Oxford history of the prison.* Oxford, 1995.

Murray, James P. *Galway: A Medico–social history.* Galway, 1994.

O'Cearbhaill, Diarmuid (ed.). *Galway, town and gown, 1484–1984.* Dublin, 1984.

O'Dowd, Mary and Wichert, Sabine. *Chattel, servant or citizen. Womens' status in Church, state and society.* Belfast, 1995.

O'Grada, Cormac. *Ireland: A new economic history, 1780–1939.* Oxford, 1994.

O'Sullivan, John L. *The Cork city gaol.* Cork, 1996.

O'Sullivan, Patrick. *Irish women and Irish migration.* London, 1997.

Oxley, Deborah. Convict maids: *The forced migration of women to Australia.* Cambridge, 1996.

Pearsall, Ronald. *The worm in the bud. The world of Victorian sexuality.* Middlesex, 1969.

Rhodes, Rita M. *Women and the family in post-famine Ireland.* New York, 1992.

Rude, George. *Protest and punishment: the story of the social and political protesters transported to Australia 1788–1868.* Oxford, 1978.

Savage, George H. I*nsanity and allied neuroses: Practical and clinical.* London, 1884.

Semple, Maurice. *Some Galway memories: A pictorial record, revised and enlarged.* Galway, 1973.

Somerville, E. OE. and Ross, V. M., *Through Connemara in a governess cart.* London, 1893.

Valiulis, Maryann Gialanella and Mary O'Dowd (eds.). *Women and Irish History, Essays in honour of Margaret MacCurtain.* Dublin, 1997.

Warren, Howard C. *Dictionary of Psychology.* Massachusetts, 1934.

Zedner, Lucia. *Women, crime and custody in Victorian England.* Oxford, 1994.

Articles

Clear, Caitriona. Homelessness, crime, punishment and poor relief in Galway 1850–1914. In *The Journal of the Galway Archaeological and Historical Society.* L (1998), pp.118–134.

Duffy, Paul. Galway's gaols. In *Dli*, Winter 1993, pp.28–31.

Forsyth, B. Women prisoners and women penal officials 1840–1921. In *British Journal of Criminology*, xxxiii (1993), no.4, pp.525–40.

Jones, Greta. Eugenics in Ireland: The Belfast eugenics society, 1911–15. In *Irish Historical Studies*, xxvii (1992–3), pp. 81–95.

Kenneally, James J. Sexism, the church, Irish women. In *Eire-Ireland: A Journal of Irish Studies*. xxi (1986), no.3, pp. 3–16.

Littlewood, Barbara and Mahood, Linda. Prostitutes, magdalenes and wayward girls: Dangerous sexualities of working class women in Victorian Scotland. In *Gender and History*, iii (1991), 2, pp.161–75.

Luddy, Maria. An agenda for women's history in Ireland, Part II 1800–1900. In *Irish Historical Studies*, xxviii (1992), pp. 1–37.

Maguire, S. J. Law and order in Galway. In *The Galway Reader*, iv, (1954), no.2, pp. 63–6.

Maguire, S. J. Drink and drunkness. In *The Galway Reader*, iv, (1954), no.2, pp. 67–70.

Mitchell, James. The imprisonment of Wilfrid Scawen Blunt in Galway: Cause and Consequence. In *The Journal of the Galway Archaeological and Historical Society*, xxxvi, (1994), pp. 65–109.

O'Murchadha, Ciaran. Paphian nymphs and worshippers of the Idalian goddess: Prostitution in Ennis in the mid-nineteenth-century. In *The Other Clare*, xxiv (2000), pp.32–36.

Te Brake, Janet K. Irish peasant women in revolt. In *Irish Historical Studies*, xxviii, (1992–3), pp.63–80.

Tuke, J.H. With the emigrants. In *The Nineteenth Century*, xii (1882), pp. 134–160.

Unpublished works

Bailey, Inez. *Women and crime in nineteenth century Ireland*. M.A. Thesis, St. Patrick's College, Maynooth, 1992.

Boyle, Michael D. *Women and crime in Belfast, 1900–13*. Ph.D. Thesis, Queen's University, Belfast, 1997.

D'Arcy, Niamh. *A history of Galway gaol*. Diploma in Heritage Studies thesis, Galway-Mayo Inst. of Technology, 1998.

Langan-Egan, Mary Catherine. *Lives of women in Galway in mid-nineteenth century Ireland*. Ph.D. Thesis, Fairfax University, U.S.A., 1996.

Lohan, Rena. *The treatment of women sentenced to transportation and penal servitude, 1780–1898*. M.Litt. Thesis, University of Dublin, 1989.

O'Connor, Aine. *Child murderesses and dead child traditions; a comparative study*. Ph.D. Thesis, University College Dublin, 1987.

Van Iersel, Linda. *Beware the flash–girls: Discourses on prostitution and mechanisms of control on post–famine Ireland*. M.A. Thesis, Catholic University of Nijmegen, The Netherlands, 1995.

INDEX